# GUESS WHO'S COMING TO DINNER

# GUESS WHO'S COMING TO DINNER

## Celebrating Interethnic, Interfaith, and Interracial Relationships

Brenda Lane Richardson

WILDCAT CANYON PRESS
A Division of Circulus Publishing Group, Inc.
Berkeley, California

**Guess Who's Coming to Dinner: Celebrating Interethnic, Interfaith, and Interracial Relationships**

Editorial Director: Roy M. Carlisle
Production Coordinator: Larissa Berry
Copyeditor: Jean Blomquist
Proofreader: Shirley Coe
Cover Design: Mary Beth Salmon
Cover Illustration: Diana Ong/SuperStock
Interior Design: Margaret Copeland/Terragraphics
Typesetting: Margaret Copeland/Terragraphics
Typographic Specifications:Body type set in 11.5 pt Triplex Serif Light. Heads set in Triplex Italic Bold

Printed in Canada

Cataloging-in-Publication Data
Richardson, Brenda Lane, 1948—
    Guess who's coming to dinner : celebrating interethnic, interfaith, and interracial relationships / by Brenda Lane Richardson
        p. cm.
    ISBN 1-885171-41-2 (pbk : alk. paper)
    I. Intermarriage—United States. I. Title
HQ1031.R54 2000
306.84—dc21                                                    00-020554

Distributed to the trade by Publishers Group West
10 9 8 7 6 5 4 3 2 1   99 00 01 02 03 04

*Dedication*

This book is dedicated to
Virginia Connor and Ronald P. Stewart,
both committed to leading academic
institutions which reflect and
celebrate America's diverse cultures

## Acknowledgments

My thanks to individuals and couples who shared their stories for this book.

Thanks also to Roy M. Carlisle, Julie Bennett, and Tamara Traeder of Wildcat Canyon Press for their skill and enthusiasm. I am also grateful to other WCP staff for their work, Leyza Yardley, Nenelle Bunnin, Leia Carlton, and Larissa Berry. My thanks also to Jean Blomquist, Shirley Coe, Mary Beth Salmon, and Margaret Copeland for their specialized contributions to the project.

# Contents

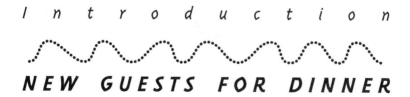

# *Introduction*

# NEW GUESTS FOR DINNER

*In 1967 when folks heard the question,* "Guess Who's Coming to Dinner?" the face that came to mind was that of handsome and distinguished Sidney Poitier. He is the black actor who portrayed the surprise guest at a dinner party given by the parents of a young white woman who wanted to meet her new fiancé. In the film, which was titled with that now-famous question, Poitier's presence and his brown skin served as a reminder that the Civil Rights Movement meant more than the possibility of an African-American neighbor. It also meant the possible addition of an African-American in-law.

That was then. This is now.

In the new millennium, multicultural relationships aren't

simply a matter of black and white. Men may be from Mars and women from Venus, but our mates might also be Italian Americans from New Jersey, or Scottish Americans raised in Appalachia, or they may have been born in Puerto Rico or France. That new guest at the table might hope for Shabbat candles at Friday's dinner or pray to Allah come sundown. Our stepchildren, adopted children, or grandchildren might hail from Korea or Russia or Watts. It's as if that routine weekday dinner has been spiced up, and every day seems like Sunday.

Whereas early generations focused on melting into the pot of American culture, there is now a growing awareness that America is a land of many cultures. Second-, third-, and fourth-generation Americans are rediscovering traditions that extend beyond religion, and are weaving them into the fabric of their daily lives. They are creating new histories with partners who are often from different ethnic groups, religions, or races; they may have the same skin tones but divergent heritages. All of us have cultures to celebrate that are far more colorful than a vague description—such as "white," for instance—might suggest. In relationships we can celebrate differences.

Some of this blending is easily visible to the eye. Consider star couples Julia Roberts and Benjamin Bratt of *Law and Order* fame (she's European American, he's Peruvian-Indian and

English-German). Melanie Griffiths' partner is Antonio Banderas (she's European American, he's a Spaniard from the Iberian Peninsula). Then there's Clint Eastwood and Dina Ruiz (he's European American, her mother is white and her father is half-black and half-Japanese and was adopted by Hispanics). Among famous journalists, Connie Chung is married to Maury Povich (she's Chinese American, he's European American and Jewish), and Geraldo Rivera is married to C.C. Dyer (he's Jewish, half white and half Puerto Rican; she's a White Anglo Saxon Protestant).

People in the conservative business world are also marrying across cultural lines. Chinese-American Andrea Jung, chief executive of the Fortune 500 company Avon, is married to Bloomingdale's chief, Michael Gould, a Jewish European American.

Of course, marriages between black and white continue, reminding us that boundaries that once defined racial territories are indeed dissolving. There's that what-once-would-have-been-shocking union of Defense Secretary William S. Cohen and his wife, Janet (he's European American, she's African American). There is also Peter Norton, the inventor of anti-virus software, and his wife, Eileen, (he's European American, she's African American). In January of 2000, the Nortons announced their donation of one thousand works of art to twenty-nine institutions—one of the largest gifts of contemporary art by private donors. This made art news the world over, yet it was difficult to find any mention of the couple's racial differences. Their interest in African-American and Hispanic art spoke for them.

Individuals in multicultural unions often find that familiarity with another culture expands their worldview. If you've ever wondered, for instance, how movie critic Roger Ebert seems to really *get* films with African-American themes when the same nuances seem to fly right by so many others, you can look to his wife, Chaz Hammel Smith Ebert for answers. This African American is obviously not only sharing the popcorn with her famous European-American spouse, but her unique sensibilities as well.

It's not just the well-heeled and famous, but everyday ordinary people who are reveling in multicultural relationships. Statistics reflect these changes. Between 1960 and 1990, interracial marriages have risen by more than 800 percent, and constitute one out of every twenty-five married couples.[1]

It's like the biological version of a cocktail mixer. Thirty percent of native-born Latinos (those born in countries other than the United States) are married to European American partners. Thirty-six percent of native-born Asian men and 45 percent of native-born Asian women are married to whites. More than half of Native Americans have married European Americans.[2]

The grandchildren of America's immigrants are part of this trend. According to a study commissioned by the National Immigration Forum, by the third generation one-third of Latinas had married non-Latinos, while 41 percent of Asian-American women married non-Asian spouses.[3]

Mix-and-match duos have gone forth and multiplied. There are now more than three million multiracial children in the United States.[4] Of course, the most famous multicultural progeny of them all is golf sensation Tiger Woods, who is Caucasian, African American, Native American, and Asian.

A vital but often unnoticed aspect of this multicultural boom are the interethnic relationships in which the couple has the same skin color but different ancestral backgrounds, such as Caribbean Africans married to African Americans or German Americans wed to Irish Americans. Since couples such as these "seem" or "look" alike, they are seldom described as multicultural. But although their differences are often more subtle, they still can be powerful and challenging. Also corresponding to ethnic differences, though not always, are the growing numbers of dual religion families. For instance, about half of Jewish Americans marry outside of their faith, and generally to Christians.

The venerable *New York Times'* "Weddings" page hints of the growth in multicultural unions. While the religions and races of the parties are almost never mentioned, on any given Sunday the combinations of bride and groom can read like a cultural hootenanny: African American and white Australian, Jewish Canadian and Jewish American, Hispanic Catholic and Jewish American, Barbadian American and Swede, and European American and Russian. It gives a whole new meaning to the term "global village."

Let's not stop at love relationships. Included in this mix are the families enriched by intercultural adoptions. In 1990, there were 7,093 foreign adoptions; by 1998 that figure had more than doubled to 15,774. Also, despite objections from black social workers, since 1968 there have been 175,000 black or biracial children adopted in the United States by white parents.[5]

As I read about this multicultural explosion, I wondered why most people aren't aware of the extent of the change. Black/white relationships seem to be the combination that most quickly comes to mind when we speak of couples with cultural differences. I was dismayed, for instance, when I asked acquaintances to suggest people I might interview for a book on multicultural relationships and was almost always directed toward African American and European American couples. The media often reflects this phenomenon. Take the word "interracial," which is one kind of multicultural union, along with interfaith and interethnic. Interracial, of course, can mean any combination of races, such as Asian and Caucasian, but to many, it's simply a matter of black and white.

For instance, in a wire story on interracial marriages that ran in the *Oakland Tribune* in March 1997, the writer and editors appeared stuck in a time warp. Entitled "Interracial Marriages Increase," this particular story began promisingly enough: "More Americans are marrying outside their racial groups, a look at U.S. census data showed."[6] From that point on, the story focused on the increase in black/white marriages, and that was it. Except for a few noteworthy exceptions, this was often the case in stories focusing on this subject.

How misleading. The truth is that while black/white marriages have increased from about 51,000 in 1960 (when they were still illegal in many states) to 311,000 in 1997, rates today remain much lower than rates of intermarriage for European Americans, Asians, Hispanics, and Native Americans. Among the 25–34 age group, only 8 percent of African-American men have married outside of their race, while that figure is only 4 percent for African-American women.[7]

One could certainly make the case that the focus of these

stories reflect the editors' biases. But the predicament extends beyond the journalistic community. Most people (including me) notice black/white marriages, because in a country with such highly charged racial issues, we have strong opinions about them.

I'm not knocking marriage between blacks and whites. In fact, I'm an African American who's married to a Swedish American. My complaint is that the exclusive focus on black/white unions is not only misleading, but it stigmatizes these relationships, somehow suggesting that the individuals, mad with passion, overrode reason and risked ruin to be together. "What about the kids?" people often ask, as if recalling the tragic Lana Turner character in the 1959 film, *Imitation of Life*. Black and white relationships are still falsely caricatured.

Underneath the cultural stigma, the factors that enter into such unions are as complex and variable as virtually any other, whether between races, religions, or ethnic differences. And the experiences of children of such marriages, though very much affected by interracial situations, are as diverse as those of other children.

This book tells of people from various heritages, who remind us of the spectrum of color and cultural nuances in today's unions. Once we open our eyes and really take in the scope of the romantic blending that has occurred, our world-view shifts: it's like watching a scene change from monochrome to technicolor.

How did we get in a situation in which Americans began focusing purely on whether couples had the same or different skin tones, while ignoring the cultural treasures they were bringing into their marriages? For decades in this country, the goal was to blend into society's "melting pot." As each wave of newly arriving immigrants settled in America, people began to downplay and even hide their cultural heritage—some angli-cized their names, discouraged the use of native languages, and renounced their religions. It was all about survival; people wanted to be as "American" as possible so they wouldn't become targets of discrimination. But Americanization has left many of us unaware of or ignoring our ancestral legacies.

Judging from the heightened interest in genealogy, and by the folks who demand more choices under racial identification on census forms, the trend is reversing. People are realizing it's almost impossible to create a self-identity based on rigid cate-gories of nationality, race, ethnicity, and religion. That would require omitting emotional identities. In the quest for self-understanding, there is increasing awareness that some of what our ancestors left behind is buried treasure, gifts to unearth and celebrate within ourselves and within the context of a multicultural relationship.

Keep in mind that it wasn't long ago that marrying your own "kind" meant finding someone of the same race, ethnicity, and religious denomination. For instance, in many subcultures, it wasn't considered enough to simply find someone who was Christian. During the 1960s, if you were a German-American Catholic like Marie, one of the women you'll meet in this book, there were many communities where you would have been expected to marry someone with precisely the same background. Anything different could churn up resentment.

"Let's face it, humans are tribal," said Martinez Hewlett, a molecular biologist at the University of Arizona. Dr. Hewlett didn't need a wall of degrees to figure that out. His grandparents and parents are Creoles from Louisiana, with roots that include Choctaw Indians, as well as French, Austrian, and African. Despite this cultural mélange, he said his grandfather encouraged him to find a girl who was also Creole. Dr. Hewlett added, "By nature, human construction is tribal. We always want to know 'Where is that person from?' This isn't necessarily a bad thing, but it gets ugly when it's a matter of racism."

Interest in one's ancestors is especially healthy for those of us who have moved outside of polarized racial, ethnic, and religious groups. I was reminded of that as I interviewed people such as the Italian-American man, who explained that his German-American wife from Nebraska had taught him to love the operatic music his grandparents had brought with them from Naples. When the couple first wed, he said he thought of himself and his wife as ordinary white folks. After three decades of marriage, he said, "Cultural differences can loom even larger than racial ones." Recognizing his heritage is his way of honoring his ancestors.

In New Jersey, a Ukrainian-American woman who is married to a Lebanese-French man, prepares for two separate Christmas celebrations—the traditional December 25 date, in keeping with her husband's Maronite Eastern Catholic customs, and later, January 6, in keeping with her Ukrainian Greek Catholic calendar. Although she and her husband are both Christians, she isn't willing to simply mix the two traditions to save time, nor is she worried that two Christmas celebrations will confuse her children. She said with a laugh, "For them it's a period of nonstop festivities."

At a home in Tokyo, an African-American woman from Detroit was interrupted during our late-night conversation when her husband, who is Japanese, announced that he had prepared her bath. On this snowy night, he had thrown open the bathroom windows, letting in icy gusts. The steaming hot water was orange scented, the room lit by flickering candles. Her husband, a director of fashion shows for top designers around the world, had revved up the Japanese bath ritual into a luxurious romantic production.

In San Francisco, a Jewish husband ushered in guests for his daughter's Christian Baptism. He is a practicing Jew, his wife, a Protestant. A week later, in that same house, their child would be the guest of honor in a Jewish naming ceremony.

In all, I interviewed 102 people, and included the stories of fifty-five. When the information is available, I describe individuals with ancestral details, preferring for instance, a description such as "Scottish-Irish" or "European American" instead of "white;" or "Caribbean American" and "African American" rather than "black." The couples I interviewed appeared to have solid, loving relationships, and there's a reason for that. Although I've included a scattering of newer couples, I intentionally sought out those who had been together ten years or more, so they could share advice about how to create relationships that last. But I also talked to individuals whose multicultural relationships had failed, for they too had much to offer, as did multicultural youngsters. In some cases, when people shared sensitive family issues, I changed their names, locations, and specific biographical details.

Like a quilt with patches of cloth running throughout, selections from various interviews appear throughout this book. A segment of one family's story will begin in one section and often conclude in another. Although the people I spoke with hail from various regions, represent a range of ages, and practice a number of different faiths, most believe it is important to recognize their cultural differences, rather than ignore them.

Married for sixteen years, my husband, Mark, and I have learned that we are so much more than the words "black" and "white" might suggest, and certainly those differences extend beyond race. For instance, people can be shaped by the cities or towns in which they are raised. In the 1960s, my Brooklyn neighborhood was nouveau middle class, with a mix of second-generation European immigrant families, many of whom were Jewish. The unwritten social rule was that if you had money you wore it or drove it (and used whatever was left over to fly to Miami Beach). Mark is from a racially homogenous suburban neighborhood in Eugene, Oregon. He would have stuck out like a neon sign if he had worn fashionable, expensive clothes. On one of our first dates, Mark blanched when he saw my body-hugging, green jumpsuit. Over the years, we've changed one another's tastes. I have come to admire his less-is-more attitude, and he has developed an understated style of his own.

There are other ways in which our differences have enlarged our lives. Like many from the Big Apple, I learned that it was acceptable to share confidences with strangers. One of my earliest memories is of a sad-eyed Italian woman seated beside my mother on a subway car, as she pointed at me and my sister, saying my mother was blessed to have us. "I can't have any of my own," she confided. Before the ride ended, she shared details of her troubled marriage. I've often said that the ease I developed as a journalist who must sometimes convince strangers to share intimacies, began with my subway and bus trips through New York City—where it seemed everyone had a story worth sharing.

On the other hand, Mark, raised on a street where neighbors chatted over back fences but for the most part kept their personal problems to themselves, was initially dismayed to realize that some people he had known for years were more likely to confide in me than him. Occasionally that has given me an opportunity to alert him to problems he might otherwise have missed, and so he has learned to appreciate my tendency to, shall we say, probe.

Place of origin, as well as race and ethnic subculture, are just a few of the contributing factors that make people unique. The good news is that when people bring their cultural differences into a relationship, it's a bit like each individual bearing a dowry—trunks laden with gifts. You might pull out an oddly shaped, battered box and suggest that this is what your family used to pave the way to financial solidity. Or maybe you'll call your partner's attention to a certain crystal jar stuffed with laughter, knowing that if you fill your house with it, the way your ancestors did, you can survive the worst of times.

The gifts we secure in a multicultural relationship aren't to be placed upon a shelf and forgotten. We can use them for self-enrichment. Let's say you hate the attitudes people in your family or subculture have about girls. So let's toss that because now you're with a partner whose sisters were praised for their brilliance and were encouraged to succeed.

It was this notion of reclaiming cultural gifts for my children's sake that initially sparked my interest in this work. I hoped it could help me positively influence our children's self-esteem. As you may already know, self-esteem in children is the emotional well within them that parents fill by giving them consistent love, affection, and positive attention. The idea, of course, is that this reservoir of self-love can sustain our children through difficult times, and lead them to make self-affirming choices.

Mark and I knew that no matter how loving we might be toward our children, if we didn't promote a new understanding, they could be harmed by the negative images of multicultural offspring. We have taught our children to love who they are, often by referring to inherited ancestral traits. For instance, our children are very tall, like their dad, who is six feet four. Knowing that children can make fun of any differences, we prepared Mark and Carolyn early on with stories about their tall, powerfully built Swedish ancestors. Our children are also aware of the many gifts passed down to them from their enslaved ancestors, survival skills that can help them prevail.

Because parents are the architects of a family—creating the blueprint by which family members operate—I was curious about how multicultural couples create and sustain loving relationships, and derivatively, self-loving children.

Above and beyond my interests as a parent, however, it was the journalist in me that pursued these stories. I wanted to see larger truths told about these unions. Reporters are taught to search out conflict to create interesting stories, and when it comes to multicultural relationships, we have certainly adhered to that dictum. That point was underscored recently when I heard about a young woman who was supposed to be interviewed by a journalist about being biracial. But after hearing her story, the reporter said she couldn't use her because the young woman didn't seem troubled.

Every holiday season, feature sections churn out the seemingly inevitable stories about the struggles in interfaith marriages. Black History Month has become another favorite dumping ground for interracial (read: black and white) couples who are under fire from resentful neighbors and in-laws. Then there's that favorite talk show topic: mixed-race children who don't know who they are.

Enough already!

It's true that many of these couples and children are at times confronted with hatred and resistance—from society as well as from family members. I don't want to downplay just how hurtful these situations can be. But I can also tell you that these disturbing experiences are not our lives. Although many people I interviewed shared hurtful encounters, some of which I've included in this book, no one suggested that their relationships or their lives had been ruined as a result. They got over it.

So I want to know, where are those other stories? How about the fun of celebrating Christmas and Hanukkah? How about the children raised in the loving protection of adoptive parents, who came away with a sense of security and self-esteem? What about the mothers and fathers who "disowned" their adult children when they married outside their race, religion, or ethnicity, but who eventually came around and feel a particular bond with that formerly shunned in-law? And if editors want holiday-inspired stories, how about Valentine features on multicultural couples who have built wonderful lives, even though they were told they were making a grave mistake. And how about hearing from multicultural teenagers, some who feel lost and isolated, as well as those who do not. One young woman told me, "People out there don't define me. I define me, and I love the way I see myself."

In an attempt to discuss the subject of being a multicultural offspring without giving folks any time for mental preparation, I asked strangers questions some might have considered annoying. Of course it was just a few individuals, but still, I didn't find any of the "broken" people I keep hearing about. In a busy shop in Manhattan, for instance, I spotted a young woman who was obviously interracial who worked as a sales clerk, and said in tones loud enough for others to hear, "What are you?" She looked as if she'd been waiting to fill me in. "My mother's Chinese, and my dad is black," she said, smiling, as if she'd been given a box of chocolates.

On a cold winter morning, I stopped a young man on Wall Street. "Half Italian, half Jamaican," he said proudly. "What . . .

your book would *celebrate* this? I wish I'd had it for a class I'm taking. Everyone thought I was supposed to be the tragic mulatto."

At a school event, I pointed out to an African-American woman that her daughter didn't look like her. When I asked if her daughter was interracial, this woman explained that her husband is white, but somehow their two daughters look Hispanic. She laughed as she told me that a neighbor once pulled one of her daughters aside and asked why she was denying her Hispanic heritage.

Days later, as I waited in line at FAO Schwartz, I overheard a cute little Chinese girl call a European-American woman "Mommy." While I was sneaking a look at them, I found this woman sneaking a look at me and Mark Jr., my blue-eyed son. After our kids ran off, I said to her, "Our children sure don't look like us, do they?" She said, "They would if we turned them inside out."

Remembering her message, that all of us are more alike inside, where it counts, I gave my children extra hugs when I arrived home. Later, I asked them if they ever felt racially isolated the way some biracial children do. My twelve-year-old son reminded me of an incident when he'd been with a group of white Boy Scouts and one of the boys had made a disparaging remark about African Americans. Mark Jr. had yelled at this boy, "That is not true, and watch it! I'm half black!" The other boys quickly rushed to his defense. Mark Jr. now added, "I like telling people who I am."

Carolyn, who's fourteen, said, "I know there are kids who do feel bad about being biracial. Maybe their parents didn't prepare them the way you and Daddy did with us. Having biracial friends makes a difference." She paused then added, "You know how in the sixties, you used to call other black people your 'sisters' and 'brothers'? It's like that for us. I don't feel alone."

She had made her point by looking back to the sixties, a time when so many of us learned the beauty of our own blackness. We needed to be grounded in our roots. If there was a drop of African in our ancestry, we declared ourselves black. This sort of declaration didn't automatically guarantee acceptance though. If the person's skin was "too" light or hair "too" straight, there was a chance she might be judged as not black enough. Generally, however, we welcomed under our umbrella, multiracial folks shunned by other groups. If one parent had a smidgen of African blood, we expected this multiracial individual to ignore any other cultural influences and raise her fists in power to the people. Anything else was considered traitorous. It was a political issue. And at a time when census information is

again being compiled, and communities will lose or gain enti-
tlements on the basis of ethnic composition, self-identity is still
a political issue.

I used to tell Carolyn that she was black and that if she ever
described herself as anything else, people would quickly put her
in her place. What a sorry, fearful message. Of course she'll run
into angry people, but that doesn't mean she should allow them
to dictate the way she views herself. Nor should someone else's
confusion dictate her identity. People often have strong
responses to individuals of more than one race because they're
questioning their own identity and what the notion of race
means. Someone might reason, for instance, "If this (white looking) person is black, what does that make me?"

If an individual's identity is formed in reaction to others,
then her identity will always be in flux, and she'll have no self-
identity. When it comes to the way I view myself, I stand on solid
ground, and I owe my children nothing less than what I had—
time to grow comfortable in the skin I'm in. Parents who tell
multicultural children how they must identify themselves are
not offering unconditional love. They're saying that only some
aspects of them are lovable; they're encouraging them to choose
one parent over another.

Judging from what we know about developing self-esteem,

self-identity is not only political, it is also deeply personal. I pray that my children are part of a growing number of future adults who will take great pride in their multicultural heritage. And maybe the world is already opening up, preparing to receive them.

Songstress Mariah Carey, whose hits have surpassed the Beatles in the number of weeks on the Billboard charts, is the offspring of a black-Venezuelan father and a European-American mother. Now a role model for children of mixed heritage, Carey tells them they are gifts to the world, reminders of God's love.

That also seems to be the message among the increasing number of multiracial models. Whether on a fashion runway or billboard, each with his own unique looks—from brown skin with blonde dreds and blue eyes, to Asian features surrounded by a wide curly afro—they seem to be thinking, "No one can tell me I'm not black enough, or white, Asian, Native, or Hispanic enough. *I* am enough."

While multicultural living is a hallmark of the Tiger Woods generation, it is families and friends who play it out on the most intimate levels. We are also the ones who decide how to view our similarities and dissimilarities and whether we will see them as problems or as opportunities for growth and celebration.

As you read the stories I've collected, I hope you will see more clearly the richness, complexity, and, yes, the reality of people who live in interethnic, interracial, and interfaith relationships. I hope, too, that this book will provide you with some "aha" moments, and help you to better understand your spouse, lover, friend, in-law, or child. If you're just entering a multicultural relationship, I hope you'll develop a clearer vision of what lies ahead. If you're already in one, perhaps it will boost your appreciation of those you love.

Multicultural relationships can be challenging, but they can also be rich, vibrant, and full. They can be a testament to the resilience of the human spirit and the human capacity to love. The stories that follow celebrate love and life. As you become more aware of the gifts you contribute to your relationships, I invite you to join in this celebration.

# c h a p t e r   O n e

# DISCOVERING ONE ANOTHER

*The early days in a love-at-first-sight relationship* are the ones we seem to never forget. Like an artist's sketch that starts with minimal lines, the details are filled in as we get to know our new love. Other people have relationships that start slowly, and include moments of disapproval or discontent. Eventually friendships emerge and love ensues. Whatever the circumstances, every couple in a multicultural relationship can share moments tinged by the unexpected. Sometimes the events shake up our first impressions or demolish preconceived notions.

These relationships can also make us feel more excited about life, as new horizons open before us and as our worldview shifts. A young man with German-Irish roots said it never dawned on him that he would marry someone who was not white. Still, he said he knew right away when he met his future wife, a Japanese American, that he loved her. He had a hard time admitting it though because she didn't match the picture in his head. "I thought of her as different," he said. But after their relationship progressed and he visited her family, he realized he was the one who was different. "I felt like some big white guy," he said. He was grateful that her family was gracious and accepting.

For that young man, falling in love with someone, including her differences, was one of those nice surprises, a moment that seems to come out of the blue—it's one of many pleasures in multicultural relationships.

## NOT WHO I IMAGINED

By the time I met with the unexpected, I had been going to a chapel every morning that was connected to the church where I dropped my son, H. P., off for day care. The theme of my prayers remained constant: I asked God for a mate who would help me raise my son. I was brought up in a single-parent home, in a neighborhood of two-parent families, where divorce was a rarity. When I married the first time, I promised that no matter what, our future children would be raised by both of us.

Shortly after the birth of our son, however, I filed for divorce. The marriage had been marked by abuse, and it would have destroyed our son. Determined not to go it alone, I turned to God in prayer, asking for a man who lives his faith. I didn't ask for someone with any particular physical features, yet I expected him to look like the good African-American men I'd always known. But I don't have to tell you that God has a terrific sense of humor.

I was in New York's Grand Central Station as a favor for a friend who didn't know his way around New York. I had taken him there so he could meet an old buddy for lunch.

As we watched a sea of people rush past, I saw a tall, handsome man wearing a clerical collar. I thought, "That's the kind of man I want." As this man continued toward us, I realized that he was the one for whom my friend was waiting, and I felt a charge of love. I didn't say to God, "He's cute, but can you send the same model in brown?" No, love came first, then I realized God had sent someone white—the man who would eventually become my husband.

First-time memories are different for every couple. Some

people told me they had long admired one particular culture and had intentionally set out to meet someone with a specific background, but that was not the case for Ralph Caro-Capolungo. A retired minister, he thrills at learning about various cultures. Still, falling in love with a woman of another race wasn't something he planned. Nor would his forebears have approved. Ralph's maternal grandfather, whose British ancestors sailed to New England in the nineteenth century, would have been shocked to discover that he had inadvertently primed Ralph for his multicultural relationship.

As a child, after his parents' messy divorce, Ralph had lived with his mother's parents, and found the wide open spaces of their ranch to be a sanctuary. Ralph might have followed in his grandfather's footsteps—only loving people who were just like him—if it hadn't been for a business venture that occurred early in his grandfather's life.

"Grandpa had gone to Mexico and invested in a silver mine," said Ralph. Although the enterprise went belly up, Ralph's grandfather returned with an understanding of Spanish, a taste for Mexican foods, and several souvenirs. According to Ralph, "The ranch house was decorated with beautiful Mexican serapes. They're blankets made of rough wool and they can be real works of art."

Although Ralph doesn't recall his grandfather treating the Mexican workers at his Southern California ranch with a great deal of respect, he can close his eyes and taste his grandmother's spicy Mexican dishes. "After school, my brother and I would harvest fruit on the ranch, and we would come home with big appetites."

With this background, his earliest memories of peace and stability connected to a home influenced by Mexican culture, it should not be surprising that years later, he fell madly and suddenly in love with Frances, a fellow community activist who, not so coincidentally, hails from Jalisco, Mexico.

The night they met, Ralph wasn't looking for love, just a chair at a conference table during a community meeting. Besides, he knew Frances. From time to time, they'd run into one another at civic events and had exchanged polite greetings. They had not been close enough to confide that behind the scenes, their own marriages were unraveling. If anyone had asked them about future love prospects, they might have pictured someone from a similar background. But as they sat listening to the speaker, Ralph said, "My hand touched hers on the table and it felt like electricity."

Twenty-five years into their marriage, Frances still sounds surprised about that first night of their love. Her first marriage had been so contentious that her Catholic priest advised her to divorce. She said in an alluring Spanish accent, "I wasn't planning to remarry. I hadn't been asking God for a man in my life."

On their first date, Ralph fixed a candlelight dinner—only he forgot to buy the candles. She didn't care, and he was too smitten to worry about details. He said, "Things moved rapidly. They were completely beyond my control."

After they wed, Ralph composed a book of original verse for Frances, recording it in calligraphy. One entry reads, "Thou hast fed me with a bread which does naught but feed my soul. Thou hast given me a way of love beyond my knowing. Thou art my love and I am whole." All these years later, love continues to feed their souls.

Another constant in these "how we met" stories is that they often occur in unromantic situations. Take the story of Roger Sparks, a European American, and Jasmin Ansar, an East Indian Muslim raised in England. They met in London. He was in the country teaching economics at the University of Essex, and she, the same subject at the City University of London. They were introduced through mutual friends for business reasons. He knew a doctoral student who was looking for a place to live, and Jasmin had a room to rent. At first their economic savvy kept Roger and Jasmin apart. He tried negotiating on a price for the room on behalf of his friend, but he and Jasmin couldn't reach an agreement. They later settled on an amount, but Jasmin's friends convinced her that this American was trying to take her for a ride and she changed her mind. That didn't make him very happy.

Still, their mutual attraction eventually overrode the bottom line. They enjoy telling about that first "date." In England, Jasmin explained, "if someone comes to your house during teatime, you offer him tea and if he accepts, this is considered a signal that he plans to stay, even if he takes only one sip. But if he says 'no thanks' that indicates he's planning to leave soon. Well, Roger said no about the tea, but he stayed four hours."

He interrupted laughing. "That's another of her cultural traits, exaggeration. Every time she tells this story, the length of time I stayed keeps growing. It was actually a half-hour."

"It was not," she interjected. "Anyway, I'd never had any-one not accept tea and stay that long."

However long the time, when it was over, Roger tried to cal-culate their height differences—he's six feet tall, she's five—so he could sneak a kiss. Unfortunately, he undercalculated, and kissed the door instead of her mouth. He rushed off. Jasmin was left thinking him rather odd.

He would eventually learn to adjust to their height difference. They have been married for a dozen years and are the parents of twin girls.

 ## LAUGHING AT OURSELVES

It doesn't take long, once you get involved in a multicultural relationship, to realize that a good sense of humor is essential. That's because we enter these unions with the same societal stereotypes and prejudices just about everyone else has. When we laugh at ourselves, we can see how ridiculous our prejudices were in the first place. Let me give you an example from my own life.

A few months into my courtship with Mark, when I was working in Oakland California, Mark flew in from New York to visit. I planned a party so he could meet my friends. Once he arrived, our differences began to surface. First of all, he was shocked that the party wouldn't begin until II P.M. He wondered how, if we didn't finish up until four or five A.M., we would be able to make church the next morning. (Church, after dancing all night?)

Then, as my old friends began phoning for directions to the party, I was excited about hearing from them and occasionally lapsed into black English. You may already know that many African Americans are bilingual. That is, we can converse in King's English when necessary, but when we're among our own folks, black English denotes a certain comfort level. But at the end of one of my calls, Mark asked, "What language were you speaking?"

As the evening progressed, I grew more concerned about our cultural differences. Mark had been raised in a Christian church that discouraged dancing. In my earliest years, I attended a black southern Baptist church that even encouraged dancing during religious services. Although he had moved beyond his most conservative childhood strictures, dancing didn't come easily to him, or so I assumed. As the clamor grew, I joined friends on the dance floor, while Mark remained engaged in conversations with another group of my buddies.

At one point, I led a line of dancers while chanting: "Your house, your house, your house is on fire!" I looked up and saw Mark was still conversing. His lack of response to the music stood in such sharp relief to my gaiety that I wondered if we were a good match.

That next afternoon some friends dropped by to help me clean up, and when we had finished, we sat in the backyard discussing how much fun we'd had. Sensing the tension between me and Mark, one of my girlfriends jokingly told him, "Don't worry about last night. Everyone knows white folks can't dance."

With a forced smile, Mark left the table. A few minutes later, we heard music blasting. Someone had turned on the stereo, pulled it near an open window, and was playing one of my favorite Nigerian dance records. The next thing we knew, the back door smashed open and out came Mark with my son, H. P., who was four at the time, sitting on his shoulders. They looked as if they were about to perform some acrobatic stunt. But Mark intended to dance.

He took one step, then another, then several more. With his hips swinging and my son snapping his fingers to the beat, this man was getting down. It was like watching a movie hero transform from Bill Gates to John Travolta in *Saturday Night Live*.

For a few seconds we sat in shocked silence. Then we all clapped and laughed, not at him, but at ourselves for our foolish assumptions. After executing a few James Brown splits, Mark bowed and was met with a burst of applause. We were all, including Mark and my son, laughing so hard that some of us cried.

Over the years, laughter has played an important role in our relationship. There even have been evenings when our children have asked us to stop laughing because they could hear us from their rooms and we were keeping them awake. I'm not suggesting that our relationship is one uninterrupted laughfest, but humor does cool anger, soothe disappointment, and is a powerful aphrodisiac.

As a descendant of people who used humor in Africa to defeat enemies and entertain friends, a people who later used humor as therapy to survive captivity, I'm grateful for this ancestral treasure. As for Mark's sense of humor, it too survived a long voyage—two generations earlier from Sweden. Grappling with the loss of the familiar, his grandparents must have sensed that laughter would be their salvation. Humor is spirit within us. Today, Mark and I, like tinder in a dark forest, create sparks that lighten our lives. Sometimes I imagine our final time together, when I'm a little old lady taking my last breath, and Mark is holding me, whispering, "Babe, I had the time of my life with you." Once, when I told him of this romantic scenario, I concluded by saying, "So I hope *I* die before you."

"I hope you do, too," he said . . . Our laughter continues.

Realizing the role that humor has played in our lives, I wondered whether other multicultural couples also view laughter as a balm that soothes relationships. When I asked Mark's Aunt Inge, who is German, she said it wasn't until years later that she realized how hilarious the early years of her marriage had been. At the time, it all seemed very serious to her, and it should have.

She and her future husband were surrounded by tragedy. She was eighteen when she fell in love with Harold, an American GI stationed in her German town, at the end of World War II. Their relationship developed slowly: she spoke limited English and he, halting German.

Once they decided to marry, however, it took months to get his base commander's permission. Inge's family had to be investigated to ensure that they hadn't collaborated with the Nazis. She was getting tired of waiting, when one day, midweek, the doorbell rang; it was Harold saying they had just a few days to plan and execute the wedding, or they would have to start the process over again.

Their Catholic wedding was held on a Sunday, and for their short honeymoon, they had accepted an invitation from friends who owned a farm with guest rooms. So right after the ceremony, Harold and Inge took off, and arrived at the bed and breakfast at 9 P.M. "Everybody was waiting, including the local priest, and we all celebrated until 3 or 4 in the morning," Inge reminisces.

When she and Harold finally reached their bedroom, they

immediately went to sleep in the big old-fashioned bed, with its high spring mattress and wrought-iron headboard. But Inge woke at dawn. "I thought it was kind of tacky to sleep in. After all, this was a farm and everyone, except for us, was already awake. So I went downstairs, through the hallway, then through a little room beside the wood stove. It was there that I found the granny of the family—she had her rosary beads out and tears were streaming from her eyes. She'd obviously been there for a while. She was so upset, it took time to discover why she was sobbing."

Inge learned about a custom that some people in her country still observed. "Before we arrived, they had followed the old practice of mounting a cowbell under the mattress of newly-weds. When the bell rings, the rest of the family knows the marriage has been consummated and they can sleep well. But the bell hadn't rung for me and Harold, so this woman had been praying for us all night long."

Inge promptly marched upstairs, where Harold was snoring away, bent over him, palms pressed into the mattress, and shook the bed until the bell began to clang and clang. "I gave it a minute, went downstairs, and there was the grandma, so happy and smiling, crossing herself. For her, the marriage was sealed."

In addition to *I Love Lucy* slapstick, Inge and Harold's early days together were filled with cultural misunderstandings. After Harold ended his tour of duty, he went ahead of Inge to prepare a home for them in the United States. He was waiting with his mother when Inge stepped off the plane.

"I walked out of the airport and saw the parking lot. I had never seen that many cars. I looked at them, wondering where they had all come from. I felt as if I were in shock. At that time, Germany was about twenty years behind the U.S. Because of the war, there was little left in my country."

Right away, she knew her English would be a problem. "There was so much I couldn't understand. In school I'd learned Oxford English, not slang. I heard my mother-in-law say that someone couldn't cut the mustard. I'd never heard that term. I pictured mustard and a knife and wondered if I'd be able to cut it."

Inge hadn't heard that among the popular services available were trucks with big sprinklers mounted on them—for the purpose of irrigating farmland. "On this ride from the airport, we passed a billboard that said: 'Rain for Rent.' I thought, 'Oh please, God, don't let the Americans own the rain too.'" Inge laughed as she finished her story, recalling her early days as a bride. Laughing is something she believes couples should do a lot of together.

I heard another story involving a sense of humor, but in this one, the humor almost kept the relationship from getting off the ground. You see, only one of the individuals was making jokes; the object of his affection wasn't laughing.

Skip Vellum, a contractor, and his wife, Katherine, an attorney, met at Stanford University a decade ago. Their early conflict was actually rooted in their different communication styles. Katherine is Filipino American, her husband, who is white, is of Scottish descent. The younger son of a well-to-do, educated family, Skip said the conversations in his childhood home "were filled with plays on words and double entendres."

Katherine, the serious and determined daughter of working-class Filipinos, was taught to take quite literally everything that was said. "I wasn't equipped to deal with dry humor," she said. "It seemed as if he talked backward."

As undergraduates, Katherine rented space in an apartment, and she and Skip shared a bathroom. They occasionally ran into one another while waiting their turns, and true to form, Skip tried to charm her with his "jokes." Rather than laughing, she fumed, and eventually became convinced that he was racist.

When I interviewed them, I was reminded that not even long-term marriage changes an individual's basic personality.

Katherine and Skip explained that when they met, she was quite innocent. In contrast, according to Katherine, "Skip had lots of women."

"Barely enough," he said.

Continuing their story, Katherine said she became so convinced he was insensitive that she was astounded when in a conversation he said he had been upset that his girlfriend had dumped him. She added, "I was even more shocked to learn this woman was Mexican." She found herself feeling sorry for his loss.

At that point in the interview, I asked them, "How did you two move past that one nice moment?"

"We keep hoping for another one," Skip quipped.

The next nice moment in their relationship didn't actually occur for a while. Skip, who had grown disillusioned with college, dropped out and did some traveling. Katherine went east for her field work, and when Skip's sister heard he was headed Katherine's way, she encouraged him to look up their old acquaintance.

"I remembered that she was gorgeous," Skip said.

Their time together that weekend led to their first serious conversation. Skip's brother was about to divorce, a situation that deeply saddened Skip.

Katherine recalled, "I discovered how old-fashioned Skip actually was about marriage, and that he was a man of great faith." Throughout the next few years they continued to meet. For Skip, the relationship was so serious that, at one point, he sold his cowboy boots so he would have money to take Katherine to a show and dinner.

Still, she said, because of his jokes, "When I went out with him, I didn't think of it as a date."

When she is asked how Skip finally convinced her he was the man for her, Skip cut her off before she could respond and said, "I seduced her." Katherine burst into peals of laughter, "Oh, Skip," she said, and the tone of her voice said it all: his charm is still his irrepressibility.

Skip explained that he began urging Katherine to move to Connecticut with him. I commented, "That must mean Skip had created a more stable life, right?"

He said, "Katherine had $300, who needed work?"

When they finally married, their families were delighted. I asked him what kept him going all that time, why he continued to pursue Katherine, and he said, "She is a complete human being."

"What a nice thing to say," she sighed.

"I won't do it again," he assured her.

Since there are so many differences among multicultural couples, you have to wonder how they recognized that they would be right for each other. The answer, it seems, is that these people see past the distinctions and discover that they have found partners whose souls mirror their own.

For example, Ikuro Alexander, thirty-four, a restaurateur, grew up grappling with her ethnic identity. She is the product of a Japanese-American mother and a father of Scottish-Welsh descent. But Ikuro's dad doesn't look a bit WASPish. His great-grandmother had an affair with a Native American, and the children born of that relationship had blue eyes and coarse black hair.

This blend of Native American, Scottish-Welsh and Japanese shows itself in Ikuro. She has been taken for a Latina, Native American, and Asian. From an early age, her ethnic identity caused her some distress. Children made fun of her and often tried to beat her up. As she grew older, she found that the only students who accepted her at her diverse Washington, D.C., school were Latinos and African Americans. "I learned to be suspicious of whites and Asians," she said. "I had black friends who would protect me from older, more aggressive kids."

By adulthood, she spoke fluent Spanish, and in 1984, she began taking a salsa class. Then, during a visit to a Latin dance club in New York, Ikuro found herself dancing with partners who, she said, had no rhythm. She was about to leave when word got around that a boatload of Brazilian sailors had just arrived, and she figured she could find a Spanish-speaking partner with some rhythm. Sure enough, along came her prince—but the encounter wasn't quite what she had hoped for. "I came face to face with this beautiful dark brown man. He looked Brazilian or Puerto Rican. I said, "Quieres bailar conmigo?" (Do you want to dance?) He went, 'Huh? Sorry, I don't speak Spanish.'"

Ikuro again invited him to dance, this time in English, but he said, "I don't know how to dance to this kind of music." Ikuro figured he was lying, that he didn't want to dance with her, so she moved away. Later, when this Spanish-looking-no-Spanish-talking man kept walking past her table, she noticed he was "cute" and thought, "I'll just have to give him Puerto Rican lessons."

But the musicians had finished their set. Ikuro was about to leave when the stranger asked her to stay, saying he wanted her to meet his dad. "He's with me," he added.

Ikuro was thinking, "What's his problem? Three o'clock in the morning and he's out with daddy."

The stranger said his father had just finished work.

Ikuro's thinking, "Great, his dad is the janitor." Her annoyance increasing, she stood to leave, then looked into this young man's eyes—an easy feat since he's as petite as she is—and noticed something. "I felt I could see to the core of his being. He looked so vulnerable. I fell in love with him."

Finally his father approached. He was the band leader that Ikuro had come to hear, one of the world's best known Latino musicians. "I couldn't believe it," Ikuro said.

Weeks later, as she and her new beau, Jimmy, got to know one another, she wondered how he had grown up in a home with a Latino musician and not learned how to speak Spanish. She discovered that Jimmy had been another misfit.

A century before, in Latin America, his wealthy paternal great-grandfather had an affair with his cook, who was of African descent. Because of oppressive discrimination, this cook's children, who had their father's light skin, refused to eat at the same table with her. Generations later, Jimmy's father married a Latina woman who tried to pass herself and their seven children off as Caucasian. But Jimmy certainly didn't look white. He has his paternal great-grandmother's dark complexion. As Jimmy's father's career prospered, his wife had convinced him to move the family out of a predominantly Latino community to a predominantly white, wealthy one. Jimmy's white schoolmates taunted him and beat him up for looking different. Looking back, Ikuro realizes that on the night she and Jimmy met, she was struck by the look in her future companion's eyes; they mirrored her own vulnerability.

After sixteen years, they have learned to bolster one another's confidence. Today Ikuro is happy that their teenage son is taking a salsa class. After all, music led her to her soul mate. She said of her son's dance lessons, "Maybe he'll meet a nice girl."

A nice girl is precisely what Arthur Bonadonna was looking for when he met his future wife, Marie. When he first saw her he knew she was his soul mate. They were both Roman Catholics raised in European-American families, but, as they later realized, their childhood experiences were so dissimilar they might as well have been raised in different countries.

Arthur's maternal grandparents immigrated to Philadelphia from a small town in the province of Genoa, Italy. He was raised in an Italian neighborhood. His family had a decidedly Old World cast. "Of the thirty kids in my class, two were Chinese, two were Irish, and the rest Italian. Only four kids didn't have a vowel at the end of their last names," said Arthur.

As a teenager, his first job was in a local five-and-dime

store. "When they hired one of their first Chinese employees, I taught her to count change in Italian. The nuns that taught us at school were imports from Italy. My priest was from Torino. You'd hear nothing but Italian spoken. I'm told my first language was Genoese. I didn't speak a lot of English until I went to school."

Arthur's future wife was being raised on Nebraska farmland, where her father struggled to erase any hint of German from his speech. They were such staunch Catholics that when, as a young woman, Marie's mother had fallen in love with a German American who was Lutheran, her brother threatened to kill him and her father warned that he would throw her out. Same ethnic background or not, marrying outside one's religious denomination was taboo.

Marie said, "There was an invisible line drawn down the center of Cheyenne County that German Lutherans and German Catholics didn't cross. To Catholics, Martin Luther was a heretic. To Lutherans, the Pope had been compromised by Satan; feelings ran really high in this town." The division was so cut and dried that a Lutheran didn't buy a farm on the Catholic side of the line.

After reaching adulthood, Marie was expected to marry another German American Catholic. Instead, she found Arthur, a nice Italian-American boy. They had one striking factor in common: their disparate but culturally isolated communities had left them painfully shy. Marie and Arthur met in the early sixties, when they were students at a university that had just begun to accept women students. It had an atmosphere with just the right level of testosterone for Arthur, who hid his timidity behind a facade he believed was the prototypical Italian macho man. After all, this was a period in America when guys like Fonzi ruled, and women were called girls.

Arthur had seen Marie from afar and was impressed by her innocence—among other attributes. "I was so dumb," laughed Marie. Every year at the beginning of the football season, freshmen nursing students put on a skit for the entire assembly, directed by senior men. "They (purposefully) chose some of the most naive of the freshman," said Marie. This particular year they dressed the young women in football uniforms. Marie came out with shoulder pads and two footballs under her arms, saying, "These are the balls our boys will play with." She added with a perfectly straight face, "Of course, I didn't understand why the whole assembly was laughing."

From the audience, Arthur saw Marie flush to her roots and realized she was as shy as he. He had to meet her. But although he intentionally ran into her at the next social, he was too bashful to ask her to dance. She was fending off some cretin who had been bugging her all night. "I kept waiting for Arthur to intervene and ask for a dance. When he didn't, I thought, 'What a loser.'"

Maybe he just needed his car for courage. The next time Marie was on her way to class, she spotted Arthur sitting on the hood of his black-and-red customized 1950 Ford. "He was wearing his football jacket, sitting there with a cigarette hanging out of his mouth," Marie recalled.

Arthur reminded her, "I sat on my car for you." She said, "Now I realize he was showing me how much he cared. He would have never sat on his hood . . . Then he calls out to me, 'Hey you. Come here.' And I actually went over to him. Can you believe it?"

When he invited her to the movies, she rushed to the dorm to sign out, but realized she had been too shy to ask his name. "I wrote down Rick something or other," she said. She would learn his name soon enough. It eventually became hers. They married thirty-six years ago in a big Catholic wedding.

Today Arthur has become the most romantic of husbands, surprising her with flowers and weekends at country inns. They hold hands together and call one another pet names. Marie is independent and outspoken. He allows himself to be (dare I say) vulnerable with her. They are also highly social and gregarious individuals, with friends from all walks of life.

Did they change one another? Who can say for sure. What I

can tell you is that on warm days, along the street where they live, they leave their windows open and passersby can hear their music. He prefers the Italian opera she reintroduced to him; he'd always thought of it as the old-fashioned stuff his grandparents had brought with them from Genoa. She also enjoys country western tunes, like those she'd heard in Nebraska. After all these years, and three grown-up children later, anyone who knows them would say they make beautiful music together.

## AS IF PREDESTINED

Individuals in multicultural relationships seem to enjoy discussing the sometimes incredible details that brought them together. It may seem as if they were destined to meet. And when it comes to fate, there may be no relationship in which the stakes are higher than in adoptions. Such is the case of Danielle, an executive secretary, who is of Irish-Scottish heritage. She says she always knew she would one day adopt a child, and traces her determination back to childhood experiences. When she was in the first grade, she moved across the street from an adopted girl who became her best friend.

"This girl seemed very talented and very much loved," Danielle explained. "And she lived in a nice comfortable family, a home where you could toss things wherever you wanted. This was unlike my home, where you didn't make a mess and everything had its place."

Danielle became so enamored with the idea of a family taking in a complete stranger and loving her like their own, that she recalls going to a library and checking out every juvenile novel she could find with a plot that centered around adopted children.

Even in adulthood she didn't lose her ardor for the subject. In fact, before marrying, she and her fiancé agreed that for every child they had, they would adopt another. Despite all this planning, it's fascinating how fate can intervene.

Four months after the birth of their first son, Kevin, Danielle and her husband, Paul, followed through on their promise by applying to an adoption agency. "This was the height of the Vietnam War. There were many war orphans, and we felt we should adopt a child from Vietnam," said Danielle. But as the city of Saigon fell to the Communists, their paperwork was lost. This meant they had to start adoption proceedings from scratch. Months passed, and as their name moved closer to another match, there was a crash of a U.S. government plane that had been air-lifting hundreds of Vietnamese babies—everyone on board was killed.

It seemed it would be years before Danielle and Paul would get their second child, depriving Kevin of a chance to grow up with a sibling who was close in age. Exasperated, Danielle and Paul eagerly agreed when their social worker suggested that they add their name to a list for children from several different countries. But the wait for infants was so long, the social worker explained, it would take about two years to locate a child.

Danielle and her family prepared to get on with their lives. "My husband was considering law school and we were just about to take off for vacation," she recalled. Only a few months had passed, but they received a call from the social worker. She said, "You have a baby girl. If you still want her, you can pick her up on Wednesday. And by the way, she's black."

Danielle sat cradling the phone for a matter of seconds, but it must have seemed the minutes were marching by in single file. Let's face it, there was a lot to consider. She was twenty-eight, had a one-year-old son playing in the other room, and she and her husband are European American. They had taken some antiracism workshops, but who could say that had done the trick. And she couldn't help but wonder how her life would change if she became the white mother of a black baby. Were they really ready for this?

In reality, it took her a few seconds to decide, and ditto for Paul. Four days later they were holding their baby girl, Stephanie. "She was so beautiful," Danielle recalled. She did change their lives, some of it in extremely difficult ways. Danielle's father, who was very much opposed to the adoption for racial reasons, was the cause of much discomfort and unhappiness. Still, they point out, Stephanie has been a blessing in their lives, and, as it turned out, couldn't have come at a better time. Take for instance the fact that Danielle was able to nurse her. "I had not stopped with Kevin, so I was able to breast-feed her," Danielle said. It was just the sort of bonding she felt her new baby girl needed. Years down the road, Stephanie tracked down her biological mother, a European-American woman, who matched her adopted mother's physical description. Stephanie was unable to locate her biological father, an African man. She learned that both of her mothers had been college athletes. And they are alike in another, more painful manner. Stephanie's biological mother's father is so racist, that Stephanie learned "it was not even an option for her to keep me. She was determined to get me out of that hateful situation."

I asked Stephanie, now twenty-seven and working as a

pediatrician, whether she thought fate had intervened in her life. "I have no doubt that I'm where I was supposed to be," she said. "When you're adopted, you wonder, 'Why these people? Wasn't it completely arbitrary? My [adopted] dad is very insistent in saying, 'On the contrary, you were planned from the beginning.' I feel I'm just part of a bigger plan.'" If so, it was a plan set into motion decades before, when little Danielle made friends with a neighbor who happened to be adopted.

In love relationships, too, it often seems that people are predestined to be together. Such is the case of Bob and Ritchie Two Bulls. Bob is an Oglala Lakota Indian. His parents and his grandparents were born on an economically impoverished reservation in Shannon County, South Dakota. Ritchie is of Irish and Scottish descent, the granddaughter of Appalachian mountain people who started out dirt poor and grew wealthy as entrepreneurs.

Bob, whose family was one of only three Native American families in a predominantly white working-class housing development, was so often harassed by the white kids at school that as a youngster, he said, "I thought that was what you did at school, fight." As he grew older, he got angrier and downright insulted by the spurious American history he was taught at school. Bob eventually dropped out of high school.

In contrast, Ritchie, a doctor's daughter in Augusta, Georgia, enjoyed all the privileges of her station. She attended a private college, studied abroad, and eventually earned a master's degree. Bob was working as a carpenter when his dad told him about a church program based in Washington, D. C., where he could live in a community setting and help people who were less fortunate. The other volunteers would have college degrees, his dad explained, but he urged him to take it anyway, and Bob agreed to give it a try. Fate seemed to be bringing the couple together.

Ritchie had joined the same program, and was asked to pick up Bob from the airport. On the way home, they stopped at a Roy Rogers restaurant. Ritchie said, "I was in a hippie skirt, drinking diet Coke. Bob ordered all this food, bent over and shoveled it in. He was a fifteen-cup-of-coffee-and-pack-and-a-half-of-cigarettes-a-day kind of guy. I didn't find him all that attractive."

She had only dated white guys in the past, and Bob didn't date at all. He said, "I was a real introvert, very shy, more happy to have a life by myself. I saw the world as 'Us' [Natives] and 'them' [white people]. Ritchie tended to be more open to people."

As the only volunteers in this religious community who didn't have family in the area, Bob and Richie were left together on the weekends. "We took these long walks all over the city," recalled Ritchie. Their conversations often lasted until the sun came up.

They were not supposed to be dating. Their religious community was loosely structured around the Benedictine Order; intimacy with any particular member was a problem. Their relationship was revealed during a monthly meeting, and while they were allowed to remain, they agreed to continue honoring the community's celibacy policy. This gave them a chance to become deeply committed to one another.

Ritchie said, "We became best friends, and we honestly feel we were given to each other as gifts." They dated four years before marrying. In the meantime, Bob returned to school, eventually earning a bachelor's degree in American history, specializing in federal Indian policy. Today he is studying to become a clergyman. His wife, he said, has taught him to be more open and trusting toward people. They have two young children.

Ritchie recounts with fondness the blessing of their wedding. It was held at the Oglala Lakota reservation community church, where Bob's father had attended as a child, and where every guest was a member of his family and of the parish. They gave Ritchie a native name, Pretty Cedar Creek Woman.

Before the service, Bob's aunts and cousins gathered around Ritchie and blessed an eagle's feather, holding it in seven directions: north, south, east, west, toward the earth, sky, and the "center," which is her heart. The eagle plume was tied to her hair. As she joined hands with Bob, they felt around and through them, the presence of their ancestors—Scottish, Irish, and Oglala Lakota—and knew that, indeed, fate had brought them together.

An infant and a family joined by a chain of events that began with neighboring school girls; a wealthy European-American graduate student and an impoverished Native American, both determined to help those who are less fortunate. Did they meet by chance? Some people don't believe in fate; they refer to God or the forces of the universe, or even coincidence. Whatever it is that draws us to people who are so different and who eventually become so dear, we often find ourselves grateful for those early days of the unexpected. The only period that can top these precious days is when you finally realize that you are no longer a single, but are officially a part of a couple. In the next chapter we'll see how multicultural couples negotiate the courtship stage.

# *C h a p t e r   T w o*

# *GETTING RELATIONSHIPS GOING*

*You have moved past that moment* of instant recognition or turned the corner from friendship to full-blown love. Now, before you can settle into the relationship, there are bumps and sudden turns on the course to lasting love.

In multicultural relationships there is more than the usual challenge of going from being single to sharing a life with someone else. If family history is any indication of who we are, it stands to reason that the more diverse the backgrounds of two individuals, the greater the challenge of remaining together. Keep in mind, however, that exterior differences can sometimes mask similarities, and matching exteriors can mask differences. The latter is especially evident when you note that people of the same race and from similar backgrounds get married every day and are no more successful at remaining together than anyone else.

So what's the secret for success in maintaining multicultural relationships? Quite a few couples mentioned the importance of facing the reality that there may be significant differences to overcome. Listen to the words of one wife about the importance of not trying to sweep differences under the rug. "Getting to a point where I actually understood my husband and his family was like learning a new language from a teacher who's on a speeding train that's moving in the opposite direction." She should know. A devout Catholic, her ancestral roots are French, while her husband of fourteen years is Egyptian and was raised as a Moslem.

"I hadn't been married to anyone else before this," she continued, "but my guess is that if two ethnically homogenous people are together, they can second-guess for one another, fill in the gaps, understand the emotions behind the words. For someone in a marriage with major differences, you have to learn new emotional patterns, syntax, the grammar of meaning. It's a Gestalt switch."

Despite some exceptional challenges, many of the couples I interviewed felt multicultural relationships were opportunities for growth and change. In fact, when asked about the challenges, two women said something that echoed my own sentiments: They like who they've become as a result of their relationships.

When you're in love, you are often willing to make major changes, and not just surface alterations, but the way you relate to the world. Whether it's a marriage you're entering or a new family, multicultural relationships can shape you in unusual and often delightful ways.

## ᶺᴧᶺ COURTING RITUALS ᶺᴧᶺ

Twenty-eight-year-old Kevin, a German American, has given a lot of thought to the ways in which he has been shaped by his multicultural family. "I'm not one of those guys who works real hard at trying to impress women," he said. Kevin has found that women who are attracted to him appreciate that he's a sensitive kind of guy. Yes, he realizes the word "sensitive" is fodder for comedians, but for him it's a hard-won trait.

A graduate of a small southern college, he said a teacher once described him as a SNAG. "That means, Sensitive New Age Guy, and I'm proud of that," Kevin added. "The teacher figured out that I never date girls just because they're cute or popular, only if they have something worthwhile inside to offer."

Now an advertising director, Kevin credits his early wisdom to a close relationship with his adopted sisters, Sarah and Stephanie, who are African and European American. He also has a younger biological brother. Kevin's sensitivity training began in his earliest years. He said, "From an early age I remember people staring at us. We lived in rural Iowa, and my parents, who are white, have these two brown children, and me and my brother. We'd go into redneck restaurants, people would stop and heads would turn." Even today, he said, "If I go into a restaurant with my dad and one of my sisters, the waiters automatically assume my dad and I are related and that she's not in the family."

These kinds of reactions have convinced Kevin that he should put more energy into celebrating differences, rather than going along with societal pressure and stigmatizing differences. He said, "I've always believed that the best parts of a relationship are the differences and the ways in which you work them out. A lot of other people think that if they have found the right individual, they should never have an argument with that person. I believe working through the difference is how you build a strong foundation. It's not the differences that keep you apart; its the differences that you can build on that can keep you together."

If he's correct, another advantage to committed multicultural relationships is that if there are enough differences, once we work them out, we've created a foundation that can sustain us during the most difficult times. But before we can become a couple we must survive courtship. Though it sounds old fashioned, it also sounds accurate.

During the early stages of a relationship, we are on trial. Picture yourself on the witness chair, with teams of attorneys presenting both sides of the case. The attorneys are family members, friends, and the occasional passersby anxious to speak up. And there's your lover, taking it all in before he or she delivers a verdict. No wonder courtships can cause us to act irrationally. As fear surfaces, we might try to conceal differences, and that's a mistake I made about our religious differences. Mark and I were both Christians, but our worship styles were quite different.

When I met Mark, I had no idea what an Episcopalian was, nor did I think I needed to know. Instead, in an effort to emphasize what we had in common, I tried to bridge our differences. I knew a Napa Valley rancher, Nell, who was active in the Episcopal Church of Northern California. Since networking is something

I love doing, and Nell and Mark were in the same denomination, when he came to visit me, I arranged for them to meet.

When Mark and I arrived at Nell's ranch, her meeting with a church group was ending, and we were invited to join their outdoor eucharistic service. In my home church, we had taken communion once a month, when little glasses of grape juice and squares of bread were passed around to represent the blood and the body of Christ. I quickly saw that the Episcopal service was different. Mark and I, Nell, and her six guests stood in a circle with the priest in the center. I was puzzled when a large silver goblet (a chalice) was passed from one individual to the next, with each person taking a sip. As I looked on, my mother's admonitions about drinking after someone else were playing in my head. My stomach recoiled as the much-used chalice made its way toward me. I handled it as best I could: with tightly clamped lips and a lot of pretense.

Soon bread followed, but it didn't resemble anything close to bread. The attending priest pressed what appeared to be a white plastic disk into my palm. It wasn't until later that afternoon, long after the day had ended, that I let Mark know how I had handled the situation. We were driving home, with me in the passenger's seat, when I said, "I don't get it. Why do Episcopalians pretend to drink from a chalice?"

He smiled as if he thought I was joking. "No one was pretending. That was Jesus' blood." Looking a bit alarmed, he asked. "You drank from the cup, didn't you?"

I couldn't answer. I was busy squirming in my seat. "If that was Jesus' blood," I said, as I wrested something from the back pocket of my jeans and opened my fist to reveal a crumpled wad, "then this piece of plastic must be..."

"It's called a 'wafer,'" Mark said, the blood drained from his face, "and it's the *body* of Christ. Please, eat that!"

Overheated and squashed, the wafer looked like someone's chewed gum, but I smashed it into my mouth and swallowed. Then, as our car zoomed past fields of grapevines, I said a silent prayer: "God, if you help me out of this, I'll learn about Episcopalians." The Lord, I take it, took pity on me.

Mark and I eventually became engaged, and I became an Episcopalian because we wanted to share the same Christian tradition. What's most important about my communion story, though, is that it illustrates how, especially during the courtship stage, lovers try to convince themselves that differences, even religious ones, don't matter. But if faith is something you or your lover values, of course differences matter, and will increasingly if you ever have children. This is a subject explored later, in "Values That Keep Us Together." But if you care about surviving courtship, keep in mind that respect is the key to handling differences.

If your mate's religion is different from yours, the best way to demonstrate respect is to quietly do your homework—reading up on the subject, initiating conversations that allow you to learn about his or her beliefs. Let's say, for instance, that the object of your affection is a Muslim. It may be too soon to even consider religious conversion, and perhaps you never will. But it would be a mistake to assume that your mate will view you as someone he or she wants to share life with if you're ignorant and unappreciative of your mate's beliefs. Appreciation is key here. Unlike some other differences, religious life has the added dimension of shaping behavior. Why start learning about your lover's faith now, when a long-term commitment is only a possibility? In courtships, we make unspoken promises: "I love you enough to understand what counts for you." It's a way of signaling to your lover that you're willing to move forward, toward the next phase.

Allen Pastron figured out what was important to his future wife, so he could move forward into a relationship. He is a white Jewish American who fell in love with a fellow student, Janice, a Japanese American who was raised as a Methodist, when they were studying anthropology at the University of California,

Berkeley. Although their courtship was initially one-sided, Allen instinctively understood one of the most important unwritten rules concerning multicultural relationships: study the person, make an effort to see beyond the stereotypes, but also consider how her worldview may have been influenced by her cultural background.

Allen "studied" Janice to find out who she really was, and it helped him win the woman of his dreams. His face softened as he recalled how he fell in love with Janice at first sight: "She was the prettiest girl in college. The day I saw her on campus I went nuts. I said to myself, that's the girl for me." There was only one problem: Janice already had a boyfriend.

As Allen studied her, he realized that despite Janice's modern lifestyle, like many people influenced by Japanese culture, she places a great deal of stock in *honne tatemae* or "saving face." This is a term one often hears when discussing Japanese beliefs. It generally applies to the outward appearance of calm and lack of emotion that one is expected to present to the public, the official stance. The last thing one would want to do, according to this notion, is lose control. At home, of course, those who care about saving face are just as emotional as everyone else. But it is the face you show to the world that matters: smooth, calm, untroubled.

The way Allen saw it, he had to devise a way to make Janice's European-American boyfriend repeatedly lose control in public. Allen's big advantage was that her boyfriend was quite jealous. "He was a real jerk," said Allen. So Allen hit upon a plan. "I was very calculating. All I had to do was wait to see them together, and I'd go up and say, 'Janice, how was your day?' I'd engage her in a conversation. Then, when I was ready to go, I'd look over at her boyfriend and say, 'Oh, hi Bob.' He'd get furious." As Allen walked off, he could hear Janice asking Bob, "What's wrong? Allen's so friendly." Allen recalled with a smile, "Bob would just fume." Eventually Janice grew disenchanted with Bob's hot temper and possessiveness and gravitated toward Allen. It may have been one of Allen's best-laid plans. He and Janice have been married for more than two decades and have a teenage daughter.

Most of us associate courting rituals with adults, such as Allen and Janice. But Ed Guerra, whose ancestral heritage is German, Jewish, and Mexican, experienced an adolescent style of courtship. In the seventh grade, he attended a tough school in an inner city neighborhood. Skinny and shy, he was a favorite among girls who liked boys with silky hair.

Desperate to fit in, Ed tried passing himself off as an African American. "I used to get real dark in the sun and I tried to wear an Afro. The girls would rub it and it would pop back to its old self. Someone would say, 'Look at that, ooh, Eddie's got good hair.' I didn't know what that meant."

One time five girls fought over him, and on another occasion, a girl twice his size sent a friend to say, "Jackie wants you to wear her chain." Ed was too scared to respond, and before he could, Jackie and a girl named Peaches were duking it out over him.

Ed recalled, "They pulled out each other's hair. Peaches's hair was in Afro puffs, and I watched as a puff of her hair flew down the street." One of the other girls asked him, "Aren't you going to fight with Peaches for hitting Jackie?"

Ed was terrified. "I didn't want to fight that girl; she'd have beaten me up." Fortunately, he thought on his feet. "I paused, then said, 'I'm not going to fight anyone. The winner gets me.'"

Three decades have passed, and Ed, now forty-one, still single and a small business owner, explained that those schoolyard fights were a microcosm of real-life romance. He believes most people are afraid they won't find someone to spend their lives with. But he's certain God will lead him to the right woman.

Unlike my other interviews, I spoke with Ed in my home, which was located close to his office. After a while, the doors to my house began opening—Mark returned from work, then, one by one, our children. I noticed Ed studying our faces. I am caramel colored, while Mark's usually pale face was tanned by the sun. Our oldest child, H. P., who is ginger-toned, was carrying his infant son, Tiger, who is African and European American but somehow looks Native American. With a head of curls and tan skin, Carolyn looks like an amalgam of me and my husband. Only Mark Jr. seems to defy genetic dictums, with eyes, hair, and skin lighter than both his parents'.

Accustomed to people studying us, I imagined that Ed was reminding himself that in a family, resemblance is insignificant, only love is critical. When he left, I made one of those promises to myself that is quickly forgotten, but nevertheless heartfelt: I'll never take this family for granted.

### ⌒⌒ *IS THIS REALLY HAPPENING TO ME?* ⌒⌒

No matter how well prepared we might think we are to cope with a partner's differences, we can't possibly anticipate every event. Even when some incident assaults our sensibilities, the best we can hope for is that we don't call too much attention to ourselves.

Take the case of Danielle, who became engaged to Paul. They are both German Americans. When Paul was an adolescent, he and his mother developed an interest in New Age religions and mysticism. Danielle was raised as a Baptist. When she went to meet Paul's parents, she was caught off guard when Paul's mother whisked her off to the country to meet Melinda Lou, a seer who read her aura. Danielle said, "I thought his mother was a bit bizarre."

Danielle went along with Melinda Lou's reading because she saw that it was important to her future husband. "I sat there as this woman went on and on about the colors of my aura." Rather than bolt, Danielle tried a more mature approach. "I fell asleep," she recalled. Melinda Lou must have approved of her laid-back approach; she gave Paul a thumb's up on his intended.

When Danielle found herself in an unusual situation she was able to "go with the flow." It's harder to be so patient when it's a long-term multicultural difference. But patience is exactly what Janey, an Italian American, had to learn about her Japanese husband's response to problems. He is the founder and president of a technology company. "He would come home, and I could tell there was a problem," Janey said. "I'd ask what was bothering him, and he wouldn't say anything. This made me tense." She said his cultural point of view was taught since he could not change what was troubling him, it didn't make sense to discuss it. But her American sensibilities demanded that if there was a problem, it had to be fixed. Over the years, Janey said, "I've had to develop faith that whatever the problem is, he'll eventually share it."

Cultural differences in communication styles can also affect in-law relationships. Witness the story of Lee and Marcy. Lee is an African-American woman; her mother-in-law, Marcy, is of Jewish ancestry. A few years ago, Lee realized that some of the tension between them had to do with a cultural misunderstanding.

Marcy felt her daughter-in-law, a hairstylist, had treated her contemptuously. Her annoyance was connected to times when she and her husband were in Atlanta, and Lee had packed a picnic lunch for them to take on the drive back to Connecticut. Not surprisingly, Lee was baffled: How could anyone misconstrue the meaning behind a carefully prepared picnic? Marcy, on the other hand, thought Lee was suggesting that she was too cheap to stop at a restaurant for lunch. Lee didn't understand Marcy's assumption.

One day, however, Lee read a story about an African-American woman who explained that whenever she went on a trip, she brought a picnic lunch. She said that even when her daughter, the chair of a department at a major university, visited, she insisted that her daughter allow her to "pack her a lunch." This woman added that although she knew the food was completely unnecessary, she could recall days when she couldn't stop at a restaurant because of segregation policies. She concluded, "A lot of us have forgotten why we offer the food to others. It's like saying, 'I hope your trip goes smoothly.' It's the black version of 'bon voyage.'"

Now that Lee had a cultural understanding of her own motives, she wondered whether there was an explanation for Marcy's reaction. The next time they were together, Lee blurted out what she had learned. Marcy was touched, and told Lee that when she was a child, kids had teased her about being Jewish. "They said Jews were cheap, and that Daddy slept on a mattress stuffed with money. This was during the Depression when people were suffering. I was critical of you because I was trying to get back at those kids. I'm sorry." The conversation marked a turning point in their relationship.

As with Lee and Marcy, some individuals in multicultural families find themselves confused by traditions that have been passed on without question and which may be particular to one family or a subculture. Others marry into families and must learn traditions that have been practiced for centuries. That was the case with Nancy Katsura, an African American who lives in Tokyo. Only a few months after her marriage, in 1987, Nancy's Japanese father-in-law died in a hospital. The next day, she stood at the door of her husband's family home and welcomed the dead man back inside. "An ambulance pulled up, and his body was carried in on a stretcher," Nancy said. Since there was no time for her husband to explain this aspect of Japanese customs, Nancy decided to watch the others and simply do as they did. It would not be easy.

That night she slept alone while her husband slept beside his deceased father. The next day the women in the immediate family sat on one side of the body, men on the others. One relative gave the deceased man a coin purse, so he would have money for his journey into the next life. Someone else tucked a pack of cigarettes beside him, although he had died of lung cancer. One by one, the participants took turns preparing the body.

Participating in this dressing ritual is customary for the immediate family, and Nancy's new mother-in-law asked her to tie her father-in-law's foot garments, which are like socks. "I heard myself saying, 'Oh no, oh no,'" Nancy recalled. As the others raised their eyebrows, Kohei guided her trembling hands through the task.

Time and time again during this period, Nancy's American sensibilities were assaulted. After the cremation, she used a pair of specialized chopsticks to pick up one of her father-in-law's remaining bones to transfer it to the urn. "It was a bone from his thigh, bleached white from the fire," she said. "I was dazed."

Nancy described her initial response to her father-in-law's funeral as feeling like a character in a Woody Allen movie, wondering if she was the only person who found the events too strange to comprehend. But in retrospect, she realized it was actually her initiation into her husband's real life.

"The Japanese take their customs very seriously," she said. "Honoring their ancestors is a major aspect of who they are as a people." She added, "If you marry someone of a different culture, their traditions are part of the package, you don't just ignore them or dismiss them, not if you want the relationship to thrive."

Not everyone in a multicultural marriage has as many new customs to learn as Nancy did. Japan has elaborate social codes that are generally recognized and respected by most of the population. Still, you'll find that even families considered "all-American" have their own customs. They can be as simple as opening gifts on Christmas eve, rather than the next morning, but even these can be quietly reassuring to members of the family.

Often family customs carry a lot more emotional weight than one might imagine. For instance, I know of one Swedish-

American family that served lemon pudding at Christmas, and relatives always knew that the individual who found the lemon seed in his serving would receive a small gift. One year, one of the family relatives rigged the game, intentionally planting the lemon seed in a child's bowl. When the "conspiracy" was uncovered, although most of the others just shrugged it off, the grandmother of the family was irritated. She could have simply been branded as querulous, but her daughter-in-law, who had learned something about Swedish customs, put her mother-in-law's anger into perspective.

You see, in Sweden there is a Christmas rice porridge which can take weeks to prepare. Crusted with melted sugar, and served with milk and cinnamon, the porridge contains one almond, which is good luck to anyone who finds it in his serving. Sound familiar? Over the years, like so many families who scrambled to become "American," this family had lost track of some of their ancestral customs. The porridge recipe, and the tradition behind it, had given way to a quicker fix pudding with a lemon seed.

Even though this older woman hadn't consciously connected the family's modern custom to stories her mother had told her of life in Sweden—women preparing the Christmas porridge, a child's delight at discovering an almond in her bowl—her subconscious memories still carried a lot of weight. From this perspective, her annoyance over the disruption of the custom made perfect sense. In fact, because this daughter-in-law understood her mother-in-law when few others did, she felt closer to her. This story is not only a reminder that family customs are emotional anchors, but that misunderstandings can be avoided when we develop an appreciation for cultural differences.

Sometimes we marry into families and discover that customs require a personal sacrifice. One woman, for instance, who married a man who is Lebanese, discovered that when there was a death in the family—including the loss of in-laws—she and her sister-in-law were expected to mourn for a year. This meant no socializing, not even a church party.

What's the best way to get the rundown on what your new family might expect of you? If possible, ask a prospective sister-in-law, or one of the other female relatives. Shortly after Nancy's wedding to Kohei, her new mother-in-law taught her, among other things, how to serve tea to guests, and she explained the meaning behind many Japanese customs. Women are often the conveyors of emotional and social information in a family. If a prospective in-law takes you under her wing, you may have made a lifetime ally.

Developing emotional and cultural understandings in relationships can help us feel more grounded, not only with in-laws but with partners, too. Ordinarily it doesn't take long to realize that our mates fulfill a need within us that we may have kept secret even from ourselves. In a multicultural affair, we can be so attracted to the exotic—the unusual accent, alluring skin color, or simply different ways of doing otherwise ordinary tasks—that it may take a while before we look back and realize that the relationship has satisfied our deep emotional longings.

Such was the case with Vivienne, a beautiful and highly educated young Parisian. She needed to discover who she truly was. On the surface this might sound like a case of teenage angst, but Vivienne's need for identity was far more complex.

Although born in France, she spent her formative years in New York, where her father worked for the United Nations. She said, "I see my experiences in New York as a double-edged sword. It was fantastic to be exposed to all these cultures. We were constantly exposed to children from around the world at the U.N., as well as their languages, foods, and different table manners."

Vivienne felt like an outsider, however, around American

youngsters. Walking quietly along the streets of the Long Island neighborhood where her family resided, the teenage Vivienne compared her life with those of her American counterparts.

Rather than attending the local school, Vivienne traveled to Manhattan to attend a rigorous French-American lyceum, an institution that prided itself on its intellectual rigor. Students carried a full load of Latin, Greek, algebra, chemistry, and physics, and from an early age they studied philosophy. In fact, Vivienne's school work was so intense that after high school, she was tested and admitted to her junior year at Columbia University.

From Vivienne's standpoint, life for American teenagers seemed uncomplicated. She said, "American girls went to school with wide skirts and bobby socks. They were allowed innocent freedoms, such as sitting on the grass and arm wrestling. At sixteen, I was still wearing full tartan plaid, knee socks, and box-pleated skirts. My long hair was worn in a single braid. I wasn't allowed to cut it."

Her parents were determined that she would retain her French heritage despite her environment. They hoped the family would eventually return to France. After several years, Vivienne found that she "had not become American but was no longer French either."

Still, she dreamed of marrying a French man. Living in the States, though, the odds were in favor of Vivienne falling in love with an American, and that was precisely what happened.

Eleven years her senior, Scott, a European-American architect, had recently returned from living abroad. Mutual friends set them up for a blind date. With his command of languages and a successful career, he was so sophisticated that Vivienne assumed he hailed from the most cosmopolitan of families.

In truth, Scott was from a working-class farm family. At twelve, his mother had dropped out of school to support her younger siblings. His father had completed high school, and in this family [as Vivienne explained], "that was like having an advanced degree."

As she later discovered, Scott was the only one of his siblings or cousins in his generation to graduate from college. He had been able to afford the tuition because he had earned a scholarship to a college in New York. His intellectual "awakening," he said, actually occurred with his exposure to art, classical music, and jazz, and the study and history of architecture. "Going away to college can create a momentous change in someone's life," Scott said. "You change, and the people you left behind do not. They continue to move in the same milieu, and when you return you're conscious of the fact that you're different from them."

After graduation, Scott lived abroad, working in Argentina, Peru, and Brazil. He was exposed to people living away from their countries, including European expatriates—Germans, Brits, French, Spanish—and by circumstance, a lot of embassy people. Returning to New York, he was introduced to his future wife.

Although only eighteen, Vivienne must have seemed the perfect complement to the new life he had created. When Scott confided in a friend about meeting a beautiful French girl, he was told, "Marry her. You can't go wrong with a French girl."

Vivienne said, "There was a certain cachet to being French. There was the mystique of the cooking, the mystique of being dedicated. We were viewed as not loud and brash or any of the stereotypical behavior at the time that was associated with American women. I was a *jeune fille* from a good family, well educated, well versed. The idea, I presume, was that an American girl would be more demanding."

Ironically, Scott was drawn to the aspect of Vivienne that she had once longed to change. She was not French, nor American, but something in between. He said, "I related to and appreciated women who were not American. There was a level of worldliness about Vivienne. She was very sophisticated, poised, intellectual, mannered, and knew so much about the world." The rest, as we might say, is family history.

They married in 1962, eventually raised two children, and are now grandparents. Five years ago, Vivienne became an American citizen, an action that she described as having a "much deeper affect on my identity than I had thought it would. I could no longer honestly claim being French. I used to think of myself as an 'ex-pat,' but I slowly 'gave up' my Frenchness—it was no longer applicable or honest. I miss it, but it's not totally gone."

She's more right than she realizes. Some weekends, Vivienne and Scott can be seen working in their garden. Their heads covered in hats that would seem less elegant on others, they are reminiscent of a scene from Renoir. Their surroundings—filled with rich colors and solid forms—are lush and sensuous, creating the impression that these two are completely separate, and yet somehow blended together.

Vivienne's instincts that Scott was the man she had been waiting for helped her make a match that enhanced her life. Sometimes, however, our emotional needs can lead us toward people who aren't necessarily good for us. That's precisely what happened to Gail Hooshmind, a European American who, in 1968, met her future husband, Hosein, an Iranian, when they were graduate students at the University of Texas. "Part of my attraction to Hosein was the possibility that he might one day return to Iran, and I could live in an exotic environment," said Gail, who was raised in Dallas.

In some respects, Gail's parents were in a mixed marriage. "My father was a Roman Catholic, my mother a Mormon. They met during World War II." Her mother's cousin objected so strenuously to the marriage, that for years, he refused to speak to her. "Although my mother broke tradition by marrying my father, both remained close-minded about me marrying a Muslim," said Gail, who was raised in a Catholic church. Hosein's parents were practicing Muslims, but he and his five siblings were not.

Before Gail and Hosein married, his mother took ill, and he asked Gail to move with him to Iran. Looking back, she realized she was eager to go. "I looked forward to getting away from home." She had been raised in a "stifling" environment in which there was little love or nurturing. So she'll never forget disembarking in Tehran. "His whole family came to meet us. They were so happy and welcoming. I went from being an only child and living in a not very loving environment and suddenly, here was this welcoming family."

Their home in Tehran became hers for the next few years. Like the houses that surrounded it, theirs had high walls with a courtyard, trees, and pavement leading to flights of stairs. "The first thing you see is shoes out in the hall, and nothing in the rooms except carpet and a T.V. At night only my mother-in-law and father in-law had a bed. The rest of the family had bedrolls. There is communal sleeping, with ten to twelve people in a house. If there were only ten, the house felt empty."

At any given meal, twenty-five to thirty people were fed. A long plastic tablecloth was spread out on the carpet, so everyone could sit on the floor, and forks and spoons were placed at each plate, with large bowls of rice nearby. Flat bread and meat dishes or fish were also served, while diners spoke in Farsi. "This family spoke a dialect from the South," said Gail. "I learned that dialect first." When she spoke to people in Tehran, they sometimes doubled over with laughter to hear an American speaking such a provincial dialect. It was like hearing a Russian speaking the Boston brogue. These were happy times for Gail. Finally, she had a close and loving family. Her wedding was held at her in-law's house, led by a Suni mullah. (Unlike some of her acquaintances who had married Shiite Muslims, she did not have to convert from Christianity, nor would she have been willing to.) Custom dictated that during the ceremony, male and female guests remain in separate rooms.

At a certain point, the mullah and Hosein came into the room where Gail waited and the couple exchanged vows, as members of his family translated for her. When it was Gail's turn to speak, the women called out, "Say yes." This is an old custom. The bride is supposedly too shy to say yes and relatives urge her on.

Only a few years after the marriage, however, Gail knew she would not remain with Hosein. By then, they had twin sons and the four of them had moved into their own apartment. Not only did she miss the closeness of communal life with a loving family, but her husband used the customs of his country, where women were expected to obey their husbands, as an excuse to restrict her movements. "He didn't want me to take the babies out of the house," she said. "He felt they would catch colds. I remember sneaking out with an American friend. I felt very confined."

When I asked why she hadn't considered before marriage what would be expected of the wife of an Iranian living in Iran, Gail said her low self-esteem had left her out of touch with her own needs. "I wanted to be accepted and to be the good Iranian wife."

As she matured, and the love of her extended family gave her greater self-confidence, she grew more independent. On one occasion, when her husband was out of town, Gail received a job offer. "So I called my mother-in-law and got her approval."

In her new job, she reported to an African-American man

who became her friend and mentor. Her disappointment in her husband deepened when she realized that he had remained in the States long enough to learn American racism. "He made some racist remark about my friend," said Gail. She realized she could not remain with her husband, and too, she had also begun to fear for her own and her sons' safety.

In 1978, public demonstrations and riots increased. The country edged closer to the start of the Islamic revolution, when religious fundamentalists would take over the government. Iran, a country that had once been considered a U.S. ally and an island of stability, would erupt with violent anti-American demonstrations. The doors of modernity were closing to women.

"Women's rights were being affected by the decrees of the religious leaders," said Gail. "My husband asked me not to play tennis in public anymore. What he didn't tell me was he'd been called in by authorities and had been questioned."

The government was cracking down on anyone disloyal, and with his foreign wife and open criticisms of the royal family, Hosein was deemed suspicious. Gail and Hosein were convinced their phone was tapped and at one point, received confirmation from a bumbling government worker. "We were on the phone, speaking in dialect, and a third voice said, 'Speak Farsi, I can't understand you.'"

With the pressure mounting externally and internally, Gail grew more determined than ever to leave, but there was the question of their sons. Under Iranian law, children are assigned to the father in divorces. Gail wouldn't leave the country without her sons, and they could not leave without her husband's permission. She decided to leave under the guise of taking a vacation.

More than two decades later, Gail's eyes tear when she recalls the night she bade farewell to her Iranian family. She couldn't tell the people who had become most dear to her that she was leaving for good. "You see, I never thought of these people as foreign. My mother in-law knew I was leaving for one month, but not that she would never see us again. It was very trying."

She had been forced into a desperate choice: the family she had longed for and received, or her own freedom and ultimately her sons'. She chose freedom. "I left behind ten years of possessions," said Gail. "I returned to Texas with my sons and one suitcase."

Worry that her sons would be taken from school or while walking down a street, and transported back to Iran, remained with her for years. So she was unable to keep in touch with her ex-husband, whom she divorced, and her in-laws. Her sons, who are now college graduates, recently packed a van and headed to California for new jobs. Gail, who is a financial analyst, doesn't regret her marriage or having moved to Iran. Through her in-laws, she learned what it feels like to be loved: that was something—in addition to one suitcase—that she returned with.

Gail's introduction to and fondness for communal life is something that Pamela Bradford would understand. She is a European American from Boston who fell in love with Randi, a Balinese, who is the owner of a bicycle-rental business. As a flight attendant, Pam often flew in to visit Randi

When she became pregnant, Pamela said, "Randi loved it. The idea of family is embedded in his culture. The family is seen as rooted to the earth. They're comfortable sitting quietly, holding their children, not overstimulating them, just being there; it's a simple, balanced life."

Their first child was a boy, and the three of them shared their Balinese home with extended family and servants. As Pamela put it, "This was a community of people who enjoyed being together. For instance, we had a large piece of property, and a group of us would go out and pick mangoes and eat them together."

Pamela and Randi returned to Boston for their wedding, but,

anxious to get back to Bali, she quit her job. Randi cautioned her, "Life over there isn't as rosy as it seems."

It was a warning she came to understand. Their troubles began after only a few months of marriage. "My husband wasn't prepared for an open and aggressive woman." He dealt with some of their differences by hitting her. For the next three years, as they had two more children, Pamela continued to be abused by her husband. She learned that Randi had grown up seeing his father beat his mother, and his sisters were also beaten by their husbands. "No one ever talks about domestic abuse there, it's too shameful. Obviously not everyone there struggles with this problem, but many do."

Pamela was familiar with physical abuse. "This was also my family history," she explained. "I suppose I unconsciously knew that there couldn't be a more perfect way for me to work through these issues." Two years ago, unable to tolerate the abuse, she and their three children relocated to the Boston area. She feels her story illustrates one of the pitfalls of multicultural marriages: If you get distracted by a lover's exoticism, you might ignore unhealthy similarities that drew you together.

Pamela said, "The exotic aspects can sometimes mask the reasons you're really drawn to him. My advice is to do a self-diagnosis about why you're so passionately in love with this person, and certainly why someone with major cultural differences. We often hope that love will dull emotional pain, but the relationship itself can actually put us more in touch with the pain. If you have a strong enough relationship, it can present you both with opportunities for healing."

Gail and Pamela's stories of marriages that ended in divorce are cautionary tales. They would be the first to tell you, however, that the breakup of their marriages had more to do with human failings than cultural differences. But how can you take Pamela's advice to heart and be sure you're falling in love with the individual, rather than feeling drawn to him for unhealthy reasons? I agree that it's important to become familiar with your own emotional wounds—and to varying degrees, everyone has them. Psychologists have long known that people are unwittingly drawn to partners with similar childhood issues, and that happens even when cultural backgrounds are very similar. People from alcoholic families, for instance, often marry people with similar family histories. When creating a family we are unconsciously drawn to the familiar. It's no coincidence that both "family" and "familiar" have the same root word. So the question should then be: When we begin to struggle over our issues, will he hang in there long enough to heal and grow with me?

Also, be careful that your determination to be with your lover is not driven by a need to rebel against your parents or society. When lovers meet with resistance, it often stokes the fires of love. This subject is the focus of the next chapter.

*C h a p t e r    T h r e e*

# RESISTANCE TO LOVE

*Everyone knows the story of Romeo and Juliet.* Even way back in Shakespearean times, folks learned that when parents try to keep two lovers apart, the couple is only drawn closer together by the thrill of forbidden passion. Many centuries later, you'd think most parents would have caught on—apparently not all of them have. But they aren't the only ones in the dark. In addition to having to deal with objecting relatives who seem to come out of the woodwork, there are also societal pressures.

Perhaps because of the universality of the star-crossed lovers theme, people often assume that most multicultural couples, particularly those who have religious, racial, or ethnic differences, were met with a great deal of parental resistance. In fact, I found that to be the case with only 20 percent of the people I interviewed. Given that this is a sampling of satisfied couples, that shouldn't be surprising. A significant factor in successful marriages is a supportive extended family (or community, when the support of family proves impossible).

When you realize how critical emotional support is to a relationship, you can understand why couples feel abandoned when family members withdraw from their lives. Among the people I spoke with, though, few gave up their lovers to maintain peace with their family members. In fact, it was usually the estranged in-laws who relented, after realizing their disapproval hurt them too. With or without support, a surprising number of couples remained together to raise children who created multicultural families of their own.

## ROMEO AND JULIET SCENARIOS

During some interviews, individuals showed me photographs of parents who had been caught between two combative groups. These were often times when I recalled Dr. Martinez Hewlett's assessment that people are naturally tribal. We humans can look for the slightest differences to justify divisions. One woman told me that her Filipino-American parents came from families that attended the same churches and practiced the same customs, but they belonged to different lodges—organizations related to particular dialects and to whom they pledged loyalty. Her parents had to elope.

Evelyn Peschetti's mother and father also faced parental resistance. "I'm the product of a mixed marriage," said Evelyn. "Dad was the first generation of an Italian immigrant family, and my mother's family was pure colonial WASP."

The English branch of Evelyn's family tree can be traced back to Massachusetts, 1635. They were Calvinist Puritans escaping the Church of England. Five years later, in 1640, Evelyn's forebears helped to found Southampton, the first English settlement in New York. Evelyn's family was not materially wealthy, but they remained proud of their blue blood. "I spent my summers at my grandmother's house in Sag Harbor," said Evelyn. "My mother would drag us around looking through the cemetery to spot the graves of ancestors. I knew my relatives in the abstract—350 years of family history."

Evelyn's father, American born, was the son of immigrants from Naples. Hard workers—his father was a tailor, his mother, a dressmaker—they had seen better times. In Italy, they had owned one of the first Singer sewing machines, and their [actual] family name dates back hundreds of years.

Once in the United States, though, they faced tremendous prejudice, not only from groups with longstanding roots, but from other newly arrived immigrants as well. When one of the children in Evelyn's father's family became deathly ill, the mother turned to a nearby Catholic church so she could light candles in her son's name. But the priest wouldn't let her in the church—*Irish* Catholics only, he said.

Against this backdrop of scathing bigotry, Evelyn's parents met as Columbia University graduate students, where they studied organic chemistry. It was 1929, and Evelyn's mother, then twenty, looked forward to a bright future. She had earned her undergraduate degree from Smith College and graduated Phi Beta Kappa, summa cum laude, and hoped to become a physician. With her extraordinary intelligence, willingness to work hard, and all the right WASP credentials, it seemed she couldn't fail.

Evelyn's father fought to keep intolerance from ruining his life. "According to the family story, Daddy had applied and applied to Columbia as an undergraduate, and they kept turning him down," said Evelyn. "Apparently someone on the admissions committee said, 'He won't go away, so let's let him in to fail.'" He succeeded brilliantly, then moved up to the university's graduate division.

In 1931, when her parents wed, Evelyn's maternal grandfather forbade everyone in the family from attending. Only his wife disobeyed. Evelyn's father eventually earned his Ph.D. Evelyn's mother earned her master's degree but never became a doctor. She was stymied by another sort of bigotry—against women. "She was discriminated against by someone in the department," said Evelyn.

Her parents' legacy to her seems clear: In life nothing is certain except the power of love. No matter what your differences or obstacles, once you find love, reach out for it.

Evelyn met her future husband, James Sakamoto, a chemist, in 1975. He is Japanese American. She not only refused to let their racial differences deter her, she reached out to ensure that love didn't pass her by. James said, "The first night when we were singing in a community chorus together, she slipped me a piece of paper with her address and telephone number on it."

When I asked if it was his intelligence that attracted her, Evelyn nodded yes, but added, "I thought he was cute." She still does. Married for twenty-two years, they have a teenage daughter.

When it comes to how they met, Evelyn and James are unlike many of the multicultural couples I interviewed because they got to know one another while singing in a community chorus. School and the office scored high in the "how-we-met" category, and that was particularly so among those of the baby boomer generation. As time progresses, surely there will be more stories concerning multicultural love affairs that bloomed via the Internet.

Before the late sixties, when women led more traditional roles, it was easier for parents to control their daughters' movements and behavior. But when large numbers of baby boomer women began to leave home for college, and eventually enter the workforce, they had more control over who they could marry. Also, the passage of civil rights legislation, which created new educational and professional opportunities for racial minorities, led to more interaction between people of different racial backgrounds.

I was one of these baby boomers. A European-American coworker introduced me to Mark in 1979. Two decades earlier, it's unlikely that this male coworker and I would have been friends, especially since I was his supervisor. Over the years, when Mark and I have run into hurtful situations—when a co-op board tried to discourage us from moving into the apartment we had purchased, or another time in Manhattan, when someone shouted "black and white together should be illegal"—I've lifted my spirits by remembering those who survived tougher times.

## OF LOVE AND WAR

Forbidden love stories are peppered with old hatreds that stem from wars, when enmity toward the "enemy" was encouraged and fed by familial and national losses. That was the situation Inge Richardson found herself in when she fell in love with Harold, a European-American soldier stationed in Germany at the end of World War II. At a time when Germans were grieving the loss of loved ones killed by Allied forces, "We had to court on the sly," said Inge.

One of her sisters, whose husband had been blinded in one eye during the war, was hostile toward Harold. "She didn't think it was right for me to be going with a former enemy," said Inge.

Knowing how her husband had been cold-shouldered by Germans, when Inge moved to the States, she expected Americans to be hostile to her. So she was surprised to find people generally welcoming, but every bit as bigoted as her own countrymen.

"In this first building where we lived, there was a Japanese war bride and we had to do our laundry on the roof. We both had babies. I was fascinated by her because I'd never seen anyone Japanese. I thought she had the most beautiful complexion and hair. While we were doing our laundry, we spoke in broken English. There was an American woman there, and after watching us, she said, 'You know she's Japanese don't you?' I said, 'I know, isn't it wonderful?' I realized the American woman did not want me to associate with the Japanese woman. She was willing to accept me as a war bride because I am white. But the Japanese woman, no, that wasn't acceptable to her. The truth was that my Japanese acquaintance and I had so much in common."

The life-shattering bigotry Inge had left behind in Germany, and the racism she discovered in her new land, made her determined to open her heart to people of all races and backgrounds. This is one of many traits her husband admires. When I asked Inge if she and Harold have worked out all of their cultural differences, she said with some amusement, "Are you kidding? We've been married for fifty years and we're still fighting World War II."

Although three decades younger than Inge, Janice Pastron, a Japanese American, had an in-law relationship that was affected by the same war. She is married to Allen, a Jewish American, whose father was a World War II Army officer. Early in their relationship, when Janice was visiting, her future father-in-law gave them directions to a predominantly Japanese area of town by pointing and saying, "Go down that way, and keep going until you see a bunch of Japs and turn left."

Determined to ignore his cruelty, Janice kept her cool. Today she says fondly of her father-in-law, "I knew he was full of bluster. I really loved him, and I could tell that he adored me. We had an immediate connection." By forgiving his insults, Janice was able to keep peace in the family.

Elise Randolph was conceived when her parents met during another war involving American soldiers. It was the Korean War, and her mother, a Korean woman, was left behind when Elise's father, a European-American soldier, returned to the States. Her mother became a social outcast for having a biracial child. With both of them facing starvation, Elise's mother made a heart-wrenching choice. She abandoned little Elise at an American missionary hospital. But she returned a few days later and identified herself as Elise's mother. One of the nurses offered her a job, and she and Elise lived at the hospital for five years.

When the American medical personnel pulled up stakes and were set to return home, Elise's mother asked a physician and his wife to take Elise with them. Elise said, "Now that I have children of my own, and after speaking with my biological mother, I understand how hard it must have been for her. She understood the stigma of being a mixed-race person in Korea."

The physician and his wife believed it was God's will that they raise Elise. But despite the couple's faith, Elise's adopted mother, who already had five children, found it difficult to accept a child who was not her own. "It was much harder for her and me to connect," Elise said. As an adult, Elise went through therapy. She said, "They did the best they could do under the circumstances. That's not necessarily enough."

Elise eventually married Curtis, a salesman who is African American. Initially unable to conceive, they contacted an adoption agency. But a friend's call brought Elise's childhood full circle. "My friend said, 'Haven't you heard about the baby in the news?'" It turned out that a baby girl, whose mother was Asian and whose father was black, had been abandoned at a nearby hospital. In a note found in the bassinet, the mother explained that she couldn't keep her baby because her family would not be able to accept a biracial child. Elise was stunned by the similarities to her own childhood story.

Although many people applied for the abandoned baby, the fact that Elise and her husband had the baby's racial background brought them to the attention of the authorities.

Whitney was four-and-a-half months old when they brought her home. A few years later, Elise and her husband conceived a baby girl. The two little girls look very much like the sisters they are. Elise said of her relationship with her adopted daughter, "I can help her understand why her birth mother did what she did, considering the racial stigma and the fear she must have felt for her." In the end, Elise feels her troubled past is actually a gift, one that will allow her to be a better mother to both her girls.

Elise's story started out sad but had a happy ending. Some stories in which parental resistance might be factor, begin on a high note and continue that way. After Yuriko Romer's family immigrated to the United States from Japan in 1959, her parents might have insisted that their daughter marry a Japanese man, but they didn't. In fact, Yuriko's husband, Bill, who is of German and Irish descent, remembers his father-in-law's encouragement during the rehearsal dinner. "Yuriko's dad spoke about East meeting West and how our wedding ceremony represented something much bigger to our families, to our culture, to the world. I had no idea. I was just asking this woman to marry me." But the next day, at the wedding, when Bill saw Yuriko's aunts dressed in traditional kimonos, he said "I realized our wedding ceremony did represent two cultures coming together."

Liane Wakabayashi traveled the opposite route from Yuriko—west to east—but this time, too, the resistance she feared didn't materialize. Liane, who was born in Montreal and raised in Manhattan, is of Jewish heritage. Her mother was born in London, and her father is Rumanian.

She met her husband, Akihiko, a shiatsu therapist, when she visited his clinic in Tokyo for a health-related concern. "Akihiko was dressed in a uniform of black baggy pants that puff out around the legs and pull tight at the ankles, with a white button-less cross-wrapped blouse. They're clothes of humility and simplicity. And I might add, they are also pretty sexy," said Liane.

She was impressed with Akihiko's range of interests. He had lived in India, enjoys Hollywood movies, and has studied classic works of literature. He has such a worldly background that she was surprised, once they decided to marry, that Akihiko wanted his employer's permission. "I told him if he had to ask his boss he wasn't an employee, but a slave." Getting this kind of permission is not typical in Japan, but at this clinic the leader was like a second father to the interns.

Agitated about how his employer would feel about his marrying Liane, Akihiko waited for just the right day and for the right conditions. Liane said with amusement, "I suppose there was a full moon and there were no earthquake warnings."

Akihiko took the train home with his boss, a one-and-a-half hour commute in the opposite direction from where he lived, and while they were crunched up on the train, hanging onto straps, he asked his employer's permission. After all that, what was the man's response? He said, "Of course. Get married, and do it soon." They did, with Akihiko's parents hosting an elaborate wedding at Tokyo's Imperial Hotel. Liane and Akihiko have been married for nine years and have a two-year-old daughter, Mirai Miriam. Like her mother—who has dual citizenship in the United States and Canada, and right of abode in the United Kingdom—Mirai Miriam is a woman of the world. She has citizenship in Canada, Japan, and the United States, and right of abode in the United Kingdom. The toddler's immediate plans, however, call for remaining in Japan with her mommy and daddy.

Like many of the couples I interviewed, the Wakabayashis enjoy emotional support from their parents and business associates. Among the stories that couples shared with me, I found that the greatest resistance occurred when one of the partners in a multicultural marriage is African American. I also found that when there is persistent resistance, this is generally from non-black parents, trying to discourage a marriage with a black partner.

When you hear of multicultural couples experiencing pressure because of war-related resentments, issues involving African Americans don't generally come to mind. Yet these struggles are war-related. It's a war that none of us were involved in, nor those born in the generation before us. Yet the issues involved in America's Civil War remain with us, for the wounds are unhealed.

A lot of people feel impatient when they hear the word "slavery" offered as a cause for continued racial divisions. After all, it was so long ago, and they often point out that many immigrant groups struggled with prejudice in America, but they "got over it." They lose sight of the fact that, as each succeeding generation of European immigrants struggled to become more "American," they were eventually identified as "white" and therefore treated with the respect (and support) European Americans often take for granted.

On the other hand, African Americans are the descendants of people who were forced to come to the United States, who were forbidden to use their languages and customs, and the only group in which there was widescale and forced physical separation of parents and children. Even less thought is given to the long-term emotional consequences of slavery, which affect whites as well as blacks and other immigrant groups. But if you're either considering or are already involved in a relationship with someone who is black or partially black, you should consider how this history will affect your life, in both positive and negative ways.

Slavery is still affecting many people because a great deal of time, money, and might went into ensuring that it would. Slavers, men of great wealth and political power who dominated the White House and the Supreme Court, had 250 years to create the most effective propaganda campaign in the history of the United States. They protected their extraordinarily profitable investments through legislation, "pseudoscience," the power of the printed word, and passionate oratory. They convinced a nation that people of African descent were morally and intellectually inferior creatures without human feelings. There were some morally upstanding people who saw through the lies, but by the nineteenth century, belief in black inhumanity was almost universal.

When slavery ended, there were no governmental programs designed to convince the populace that skin color is not a determinant of character. Instead, brutal segregation policies ensued, which reinforced racist beliefs. Since the mid-1960s when segregation was dismantled, there have been many legislative and social advancements. Prejudice continues, however, because beliefs are passed down—consciously and unconsciously—from one generation to the next. Negative beliefs about black people have also been passed on to each wave of newly arriving immigrants and have been exported abroad.

If there was ever confirmation that something good can be wrung from even the most horrific experiences, it is this: every ethnic group emerges from its sufferings with specific survival skills that can help future generations prevail. The gifts that grew out of the African-American experience include: creativity (because we were forced to make "something from nothing"), a deep and abiding faith in God, a sense of determination and persistence, strong intuitive skills, a sense of humor, and the ability to inspire others.

Still, anti-black racism continues to be perpetuated. One response to this situation is that a substantial number of black Americans wouldn't consider marrying someone of another race, and apparently those feelings are reciprocated. Michael Lind, a *New York Times Magazine* contributor, has written, "The major cause of low black out-marriage rates may well be anti-black prejudice." He further points out that a 1997 Knight-Ridder poll showed that even among respondents generally comfortable with intermarriage, "a full 3 in 10 respondents opposed marriage between blacks and whites."[8]

Negative perceptions about black people can fuel parental opposition to interracial relationships. Witness the story of Elise, who is Eurasian. When she told her adopted parents, who are European Americans, that she planned to marry an African-American man, Elise's mother asked if he was clean. Elise was taken aback by the prejudice African Americans experience. A few years into their marriage, after her husband was refused a bank loan, Elise took their paperwork to the same white loan officer. Apparently the couple's finances looked more promising when presented by a Eurasian, rather than an African American. This time the loan was approved. Anti-black prejudice isn't limited to the U.S. When Gregor Williams, an African American in Stockholm, wed a Swedish woman, her grandmother saw their baby and said, "She looks like a troll."

Obviously there is contempt on both sides of the racial divide. When Emmy, a Polish Canadian married Gene, a Caribbean American of African descent from Nashville, "his sister wouldn't look at me or acknowledge my presence," recalled Emmy.

That was only the start of their problems. Emmy was a flight attendant for an airline that flew to Japan, where Gene was stationed in the air force. When they began dating in 1968, a white pilot, irate about seeing a white woman with a black man, posted a list of crew members and wrote beside Emmy's name, "NF"—an abbreviation for a racial epithet with sexual connotations.

The situation only deteriorated when an officer told Gene, "You niggers gotta stay away from these white girls." Gene argued with him and the officer wrote him up for confronting him. The repercussions continued: Gene lost a stripe and his salary was reduced. Emmy was named persona non grata by the base commander, and her airline fired her. But she doesn't take insults lying down. She filed a lawsuit, charging violation of her civil liberties, and the airline reversed its decision and reinstated her with back pay. None of their troubles put an end to Gene and Emmy's relationship. "We had to laugh or we would have gone crazy," she said. They have been together since 1971 and have three daughters.

Tina, a business executive who became engaged to Walter, an attorney who is African American, discovered that prejudice can be buried in the subconscious. Her mother is Irish and German American, her father is Lebanese. Her maternal grandfather had objected to Tina's parents' marriage. Tina's grandfather said, "Lebanon is so close to Africa that he [Tina's father] might have some black blood."

Hurt by this show of prejudice, Tina's parents vowed to raise their own children differently, committed their lives to social justice and civil rights causes, and intentionally moved to an integrated neighborhood in North Carolina, where their children attended schools that were predominantly black. So years later, when Tina announced her plans to marry an African-American man, she expected her parents to at least be supportive. She was disappointed to later overhear her mother crying about the prospect of an African-American son-in-law. Tina heard her mother saying, "This is what we get for the way we raised her."

Tina's parents have since grown supportive of the couple, who have been married for seventeen years. But Tina feels their initial reluctance indicates that even the most liberal white people often harbor prejudice against blacks. "It's a head/heart thing. Intellectually, my parents are not racists, but these feelings are so deeply woven in the American psyche that they couldn't easily shake them."

Obviously, not everyone responds negatively to these marriages. Donald, a European American who is an executive for a Fortune 500 company and who is married to an African-American woman, says his CEO insists that wherever Donald is transferred—whether to a new country or new city in the United States—the family is directed to areas conducive to multiracial family life.

Peggy Johnson, a European American, is also thankful that her parents taught her that racial prejudice was wrong. When Peggy entered the University of Oregon in the late sixties, she was looking forward to "knowing someone who wasn't just like me," she said. Peggy subsequently fell in love with fellow student Wilson Johnson, an African American.

By that time, her mother had passed away, but Peggy did worry about how her dad would react, for all his talk about the horrors of prejudice. As it turned out, when her father met Wilson, he was true to his word, and welcomed him to the family. Peggy added, "But he did warn me that other people might not accept our relationship, so he told me to be sure about what I was doing."

There are some parents who start out resisting, and never soften their stance. In the 1970s, when Danielle, who is German American, told her father she and her husband were adopting an infant who is European and African American, her father was furious. A religious man, and generally compassionate, he told Danielle she was making a terrible mistake, that she was ruining her career and her biological son's life. He added, "I have black employees, that doesn't mean I have to sleep with them."

After the adoption, Danielle's father didn't welcome his daughter and her family to his home, and for three years, he barely spoke to her. And it didn't help their relationship any when Danielle and her husband adopted a second biracial daughter, bringing their number of children to four—two biological sons and two African- and European-American adopted daughters.

A few years into this cold war, Danielle's mother invited them for a visit, "but they tried to keep us under wraps," Danielle said. During this vacation, Danielle and her mother made a quick shopping trip, leaving Stephanie and Sara, who were thirteen and ten, home with Danielle's father. Sara said, "My sister and I each stuck a foot in the pool and my grandfather started yelling. He didn't want us to get into his pool."

Over the years, her grandfather has continued to cast a shadow over their lives. For example, he would invite his grandsons to visit him and take them to amusement parks. Sara said, "My mother's brother saw what was happening, and he would invite me and my sister to visit him and also take us to amusement parks. But my sister and brothers and I knew there was something very wrong with that picture." Sara said on the occasions when she saw her maternal grandparents, "It felt like I had to walk on eggshells because I didn't want to do anything to make them not like me."

Over the years, Danielle's father has remained unrepentant.

During a family event, Stephanie said, "The entire evening, I felt so small and on edge. I was in the room with people I love, but my grandparents' presence made me feel so uncomfortable."

Stephanie has compassion for her grandparents' ignorance, but she has learned from the situation that their prejudice, as she put it, "Isn't my issue. I don't have to take on the burden of their ignorance."

Both Stephanie and Sara feel it's important to stress that their mistreatment was connected to their maternal grandparents, not their adopted father's parents, who had a completely different response. When Danielle called to tell them they had adopted the first of their biracial children, Danielle worried she would get flak from them too, as she had from her own parents. Danielle recalls that conversation with her mother-in-law. "We had been scheduled to visit, and I asked if they still wanted us to come." Her mother-in-law said, "Of course you can still come. What's the big deal? She's brown, so what?"

No matter how understanding or supportive family members of any race might be about a marriage involving African Americans, there are other complications that might arise that have more to do with friction among African Americans, issues that have arisen as a result of anti-black prejudice, and these too have historical roots. Since loyalty among African captives was a

life and death issue, they developed a biting contempt for anyone among them who crossed the line and betrayed their secrets
to those who were in power. This sense of loyalty continues to
have a powerful hold on our people. At its best, our loyalty to one
another is demonstrated by the many people who have taken in
and raised extended family members who are unable to remain
with their own parents. But this sense of loyalty also leads some
African Americans to view marriage to anyone out of the race—
particularly someone white—as a betrayal. Two of the African-
American men I interviewed were affected by these attitudes.

Wilson Johnson, forty-eight, a manager for a transportation
company, who married Peggy, his college sweetheart, who is
European American, is bothered by the fact that some people
who see him with his white wife assume that he's a black man
who hates black women. "That's absolutely ridiculous," he said.
He finds the idea of being labeled "disloyal" particularly ludi-
crous when some of the finger pointers are highly color conscious, and only willing to date or marry fair-skinned
African-American partners.

Color consciousness dates back to the favoritism slaveholders showed for captives who had more "European" features and
who were often their unrecognized progeny. Deemed prettier,
smarter, and cleaner than African people with browner skin,

these lighter skinned captives were frequently given kitchen work rather than harsher field duty. The situation went far beyond who worked where, however. Favoritism from a slaveholder could mean that one child was sold away, while another remained with his family. Also, keep in mind that these physical differences were exploited by slaveholders who practiced mind control, the theory being that a divided black populace could more easily be kept in captivity.

Today issues of skin color and facial features are still a divisive issue among African Americans. (To a lesser extent, this issue affects other ethnic groups, including Jewish, Italian, and Latino families, where preferences are sometimes shown for offspring with lighter coloring.) Robin, twenty-nine, whose mother is white and Jewish and whose father is an African American, was unprepared for the nuances of race. Her parents divorced when her mother was pregnant with her, and Robin's mother—who worried that her brown-skinned daughters would be discriminated against—raised Robin and her sister in a commune that was known for its emphasis on civil rights. Robin recalled, "Our community was racially diverse, and there were no racial issues. I didn't know there was prejudice."

Robin left the commune when she was eighteen, unprepared for the real world. Although she met many African Americans who accepted her for who she is, there were others who made her feel "heavily judged." She said, "Some black men were pissed off if I dated a white man." A few others seemed to be attracted to her because she has silky hair and almond-toned skin. "And there were some black women who seemed to hate me because of my hair. It was depressing to find that there was discrimination between some light- and dark-complexioned black people."

Robin said she thought she had come up with the right idea for finding the right guy when she began attending a singles night at a synagogue. "I told one of my Jewish friends, 'I'm looking for a nice Jewish boy,' but he said, 'You should understand one thing: you are black in their eyes.' I realized that as a person of color sitting in a temple of predominantly white people, regardless of the fact that I am Jewish, a man might be attracted to me but feel he couldn't take me home to his family." Her search continues.

Perhaps Robin would take heart if she were to hear the story of Gregor, fifty-nine, an African American who was raised in Lincoln, Nebraska. He too got caught up in the complexities of color and race, before creating peace in his life. Gregor said, "My mother's people had been free blacks as far back as the 1800s in South Carolina. My mother was very light complexioned, and my dad, dark brown." In contrast to Gregor's skin tones, which are a deep burnished brown, his sister has light skin. Their color-conscious mother favored his sister. "There were subtle things from my mother, unspoken, but it was favoritism," Gregor said.

He ran into the same kind of bias in the black community. "There was a lot of discrimination. At parties, some girls would not dance with me because they considered my hair too kinky."

In addition to rejection because of his physical features, Gregor's peers criticized him for not acting "black enough." This may sound simplistic, but as we're learning, notions behind cultural nuances seldom are. Being judged "black enough" ties into centuries-old expectations of loyalty, and suggests that one's choices should be determined by the majority. For instance, playing basketball—a sport that attracts many lower income athletes because it doesn't require expensive equipment—would be deemed acceptable, while lacrosse, a considerably more expensive game, would be viewed as a white person's sport. The list of what is and isn't acceptable is endless. And although black people regularly resist the pressure, becoming harpists, for instance, or botanists or linguists, and so on, this cultural phenomenon continues, perpetuating damaging stereotypes.

These black-enough determinations are also products of a mindset called "identification with the enemy." In effect, this means that we can become our own enemies. After centuries of being denied access to a better life, particularly through education, some young African Americans resent those who value academic achievement, standard English, or anything they might associate with white culture—symbols of painful oppression.

Since so many feel shunned by whites, being rejected by other black people can be enormously painful. In the chapter, "What About the Kids?" some multiracial people discuss this dilemma.

Gregor came of age in the 1950s, a time of rampant segregation, so he had virtually no contact with people outside of his black neighborhood. Rejected by his mother and his community because of his skin tone, and ostracized by his peers for his interests, his adolescence and teen years were unhappy times. "In high school, I was involved in sports but only cross-country, not basketball, as many of my black friends were. And rather than soul music, I liked classical music and jazz. I didn't fit into any of the molds that were considered acceptable, so a lot of kids made fun of me. One black girl called me 'Snow' [because she felt he 'acted white']. I didn't understand black dialect, either, so I was considered truly square. When I asked one black girl, 'Would you like to go to the opera?' She said, 'Boy, you'd better get up out of my face.'"

Apparently neighborhood kids weren't the only ones who thought Gregor odd. When he left for college, his mother warned, "Don't even think about bringing a white woman to this house."

After college, Gregor joined the Peace Corps and served in Ethiopia for two years. He was disturbed to find that colonialism had left a familiar mark: "Ethiopians had the same issues about hair texture and skin color. Black volunteers with lighter features tended to be more popular than browner-skinned volunteers."

Long a fixture in choral music circles, Gregor applied for and was accepted to a conservatory in Vienna. Ironically, many of the Europeans he met gave him a new sense of his worth. "For the first time I encountered people who appreciated me for my hair texture, skin color, and physical features. I'd struggled in circles that made me wish I had wavy hair and lighter skin. I had to go all the way to Europe to be appreciated."

He eventually moved to Stockholm where he mastered the Swedish language, taught school, and married a Swedish woman. But when that union ended after seven years, he and his two daughters returned to the States, where he teaches social studies. He began dating African-American women with similar cultural interests, and he grew close to one, but they were at loggerheads over spiritual issues. "She'd had bad experiences with Catholicism, and wanted nothing to do with the church," he said. Actively involved in his church, and passionate about choral music, Gregor didn't want to spend his life with someone with such different interests.

By 1980, he'd met Kathleen, who Gregor described as "the perfect match in terms of values and cultural interests." But there was one major problem: Kathleen is European American. "I didn't want to deal with being married to another white woman," Gregor said. "There's so much resistance from white society, and some black people think you can't be truly black if you're married to someone white."

Still, he found Kathleen difficult to resist. Although raised in an affluent suburb, her upbringing was somewhat atypical. One of the most striking events in her mother's childhood occurred in the backwoods of Kentucky and concerned the ugliness of racism. Kathleen said, "Mom once brought home a school picture and her grandfather looked at it and said, 'Why are you sitting next to that nigger?'" Although children were taught not to talk back, her mother spoke up, saying, "Grandpa, I like that girl. Why shouldn't I?" Kathleen's mother and Kathleen eventually moved away from Kentucky, and after getting a divorce, Kathleen's mother married a well-to-do European-American man. Perhaps because of her childhood memory, Kathleen's mother taught her racism was wrong.

Shaped by her mother's attitude, Kathleen said that when she met Gregor, "I was taken with who he is: very intelligent, charismatic, with a great love of music and people, and a tremendous sense of integrity. To me he is a beautiful, handsome man and I had no filter to tell me otherwise."

As their love continued to grow, Gregor wondered why he was giving in to exterior pressures. "I realized a lot of what I was giving in to was just plain crap. Blackness isn't about shouting racial stereotypes. I can't try to be anything but who I am." They married in 1985, in the church where they both sing in the choir.

Gregor has reached a time in his life in which he feels comfortable in the skin he's in.

## ONE FATHER FIGHTS THE TIDE

While I conducted months of interviews before writing this book, there was one story in particular that I will always recall. It is a reminder that no one can stop love from occurring.

Linda Yao's family thought they could control most aspects of their lives, including their children. The Yaos, highly respected in San Francisco's Chinatown, began establishing their lives in the United States before the start of the twentieth century. Linda, now forty-one, and a pharmacist, lived with her paternal grandparents, father, sister, paternal uncle, his wife, and their two daughters over their family-owned restaurant. They were active in their Buddhist church, which had been founded by Linda's great-grandmother. Although the children did rub shoulders with non-Chinese students once they began attending high school, most of their contacts were with other Chinese Americans—and that was the way Linda's father hoped to keep it. By the mid-seventies, however, he read the handwriting on the wall, and for him, the news was bad.

Linda was one of four girl cousins raised in the same home. In addition to Linda, there was her sister and the two daughters of her paternal uncle. Their parents, grandparents, and aunties referred to them as "cousins number one, two, three, and four." When they began dating all hell broke loose.

Cousin #1 threw the family into a panic when she dated a white pharmacist. The network system of aunties went into a huddle and searched out a more proper suitor. Linda explained, "They find you a guy they approve of—and that's always a Chinese guy who is a professional, preferably, a doctor—you go out with him five times and soon you're supposed to start talking wedding plans."

Cousin #2 had the "audacity" to date a Mexican guy who was divorced with two kids.

Cousin #4, Linda's sister, went the approved route, dating a Chinese-American optometry student who lived with his parents and grandparents. Linda said, "He had a pencil neck and was sort of a Chinese Woody Allen. But for our family, he fit the mold."

Then there was Linda, Cousin #3. An undergrad at the University of California, Berkeley, she wanted to move on campus. She said this was akin to a battle cry. "In a traditional Chinese family, you live with your parents until you're married."

Her dad tried his standard line: "If your grandmother has a heart attack, you'll have to live with that." When that didn't work, he tried bribes: "I'll give you a car if you don't move over there, and money so you can drink lattes."

This too having failed, he cut Linda off financially. She moved to a campus co-op, where she worked to support herself. "When Dad first dropped me off at the co-op, he saw I had a white roommate and a black roommate. He came into the room and asked, 'Do you want to go home?' Then he said, 'Okay, let's go home.'"

Linda didn't even consider looking back, and soon began dating Peter, an Irish-American graduate student, who had been her calculus tutor. Her father warned, "This is not going to happen." Dr. Yao may have felt more determined than ever, because by then Cousin #1 had looked over the young men her aunties had recommended, dumped the European-American pharmacist, and married a man Linda describes as a "disco Asian." "He wore an open collar and gold chains. He was in real estate. He is too slick—six feet tall and very handsome." At "least" he was Chinese.

Still walking the straight and narrow, Linda's sister married the young man her father approved of. Linda says woefully, "She didn't forge any new paths for me." When Linda started talking about marriage to Peter, her dad threatened to disown her.

Where was Peter in all this? Off to South America, saying he just wasn't ready to make a commitment. (Ever heard that one?) With Peter out of the country, "My dad turned his sister-in-law on me, and they found me a guy. They told me, 'Come on, Peter's gone. Try this engineer.' We went to the aquarium. I confessed to him about being in love with Peter. He was very understanding."

Having completed pharmacy school, the still-unmarried Linda returned to her family home. She was still dating Peter, who had moved back to the States. "All this time, my dad had not admitted to anyone that I was living on campus. He was ashamed. By then I was twenty-six, and they monitored my every move. It was eight or nine years after Peter and I had met, and by then Dad was finally ready to give up. He was starting sentences out with, 'Since you guys are going to get married.'"

With Peter closer to making a commitment, it was time to meet his family, who lived in a conservative suburban enclave outside of Rochester, New York. "Race relations are bad in my hometown," said Peter. "There is a Mexican in the neighborhood, but he's a brain surgeon. When my dad's sister married in 1910, she married an Italian. Her father wouldn't talk to her for two years."

Peter said of his father, who started a successful manufacturing business, "My dad only went to the ninth grade, but he lived the so-called American dream. He had a Cadillac El Dorado, belonged to a country club, had a nice house, pool in the backyard, and an acre of property. He was a little raffish for our neighborhood and was a great tipper, because he knew what it was like not to have. We went to church every Sunday, my brothers were altar boys, my mother a dutiful Catholic."

Peter, now forty-three and a chemist, said he never fit into his family because he liked books. "My folks didn't know about college. My older brother went for a semester. The others went to work."

When Linda's aunt in San Francisco heard she was going to

meet Peter's family, she advised, "Don't stay with them. Stay in a hotel so you can escape when they begin to insult you."

There were a few strained moments in that Rochester suburb. One of Peter's brothers asked Linda, "How long have you been here?" Linda thought he was referring to the length of her stay in Rochester. What he meant was, how long have you been in the U.S.? Peter said, "I wanted to tell him that her family has been here more than a hundred years, a lot longer than our family has."

After a few days, Peter's father gave them his blessing, in his own inimitable style. He said, "Linda, you really are a doll and you're welcome to join our family. I don't know what the hell your kids are going to look like, but..."

They had a short engagement and married in December of 1987, with most of the three hundred guests selected by Dr. Yao and Linda's aunties. The bride wore white, and then red—the Chinese color for good luck. While Peter's parents are enthusiastic about Peter and Linda's thirteen-year marriage and their two children, now ten and eight years old, Dr. Yao remains cautious. After all these years when they ask whether he thinks they have a good marriage, he answers, "That remains to be seen."

As surprising as it might be, the more familiar I've become with Dr. Yao's story, the more sympathy I've developed for him.

Why? Well I too am a parent, and so I understand how difficult it is to let go and to allow our children to live their lives. Perhaps one day, if I ever make the mistake of telling one of my kids who is and isn't suitable marriage material, I'll have to search this story out and read it again.

## 〰️〰️ FORGIVING AND MOVING ON 〰️〰️

Although I heard many different stories of familial resistance, there was one oft-repeated refrain used to wrap up many of these narratives: "Now, Dad (or Mom) loves my husband (or wife) as much (or more than) me." Many resisting relatives moved through a process that began with disapproval, then continued with shame, anger, and distancing, then—as they got to know the "outsider"—gradual acceptance, then, in many cases, genuine affection.

Not all endings are happy, of course. Some resisters will never give in. But until they have died, you can never say never. You may recall Elise, the Korean-American woman, whose white adopted mother asked about the cleanliness of the African-American man Elise was marrying. Two months before Elise married Curtis, her parents invited them over and tried to dissuade them from marrying. After hearing their arguments, Curtis said, "You know what? We're getting married, and if you'd like to be part of that it would be great. If you decide not to, well, we understand." Elise said, "A few minutes later my dad was pulling out a suit asking for our advice about what to wear for the ceremony. I think they realized they couldn't really cut themselves off from their daughter."

Asked to reflect on her parents' change of heart, Elise said, "For my dad, who considers himself just and fair, the reality that he had some racist attitudes was troubling. Today they love Curtis. I think they even like him better than they do me. I've realized that my mom likes strong people. Curtis stands up to her. He is not going to be bullied by her, but he is such a good-natured guy that he does it with a sense of humor."

Elise is also close today to an adopted brother, who resented her being brought into the family and taunted her by calling her "a Jap." These change-of-heart stories say a lot of about how people can become closer once they see through stereotypes. Marriage or adoption sometimes forces us to know someone on an intimate level who we initially perceive as "different." When barriers are broken down, genuine affection and love can grow.

That is certainly what happened with Linda and Peter, the Chinese-American and Irish-American couple whose story was told in the preceding section. While his parents didn't resist his marriage, they had been culturally isolated in a predominantly white wealthy suburb. Linda's inclusion into the family forced members to stretch themselves, and today his family has truly embraced her.

Donald, the German-Swedish American businessman who married an African-American woman, was shunned by his parents after his marriage. Janna even tried phoning his mom. "I said 'This is Janna, please don't hang up. I don't understand how you can not speak to your son because of his marriage to me.' His mother said, 'There's nothing I can do about this.'" They both cried as they hung up.

Years later, Donald wrote a note to his parents saying that he was going to write them out of his life if they refused to accept his wife, and his parents relented. As with many families, time and certain experiences had softened their attitudes.

Not everyone is willing to wait for gradual acceptance from in-laws. Yuriko Romer, forty-two, who is Japanese American, was in a relationship with a man from an Irish-American family. But when they began discussing marriage, Yuriko felt that not only were their lives not "in sync" with each other's, she also felt their differences went beyond him being white and her being Japanese.

"I never felt accepted by his parents," said Yuriko. She had been raised in a Protestant church. This young man's father, who had come from Ireland, had retained a close connection to the Irish-American community, and the family was strongly tied to it and the Catholic Church. Even more, she had the strong impression that if "push came to shove," this young man would side with his family before her. Yuriko waited for a better match. That's what she got.

Later, she began dating Bill who has German-Irish and Catholic roots. Yuriko was initially concerned about how his family would respond to her. "I met some sibs first, then more sibs and finally his parents, and it was a big, big relief. I felt really welcome." They married in January 1997, and have a two-year-old son.

Ralph Caro-Capolungo, a Caucasian with English roots, did give his mother time to soften her stance, but for the first few years, she remained cold and unfriendly to his wife, Frances, who is Mexican. Rather than refer to her by name, her mother-in-law called her "that Mexican woman." It turned out that it was the strength of Frances's character that turned the situation around.

The forgiveness that occurred in this family was connected to an incident involving a cultural difference. Ralph has been "an absolute pacifist from a young age," and Frances had long admired his gentle manner. But she had been taught there were some things a man was absolutely expected to fight for, and chief among them was protecting the women in his life.

So Frances became enraged with Ralph during a visit to his aging and infirm mother, when they discovered that his mother's new husband was abusive. A semi-invalid, she was too weak to call for help when she needed it, and had to ring a bell instead. On one occasion her husband became impatient and held the bell to her ear, ringing it loudly. Frances demanded that Ralph challenge this man, and when he wouldn't, she stormed from the house toward the bus station so she could return home. Realizing why her daughter-in-law had left, Ralph's mother insisted that the others help her into her robe and slippers, and they piled into the car.

When they caught up with Frances, she refused to ride with them. His mother seemed to see Frances for the first time. She called from the car window, "Frances, if you leave, you're leaving me too," and she cried. The two women rode home together in companionable silence.

Why would Frances risk her marriage for a woman who spurned her? She said, "In my country the mother is revered. I remember as a girl, my grandmother coming to live in our house when she was dying. No one ate in that house before my grandmother ate. Whatever was prepared for her was done with such love."

Influenced by these memories, after her mother-in-law's health continued to decline, Frances refused to consider placing her in a rest home. Ralph said, "Frances insisted that my mother come to live in our house. These are the memories I have of them together. Before her death, Mother may have been feeble, but she knew she was loved by Frances, and she loved her in return."

Of course, not everyone can be as kind-hearted as Frances. But she can serve as a role model, reminding us that if we respond to hatred with hatred, we will only create more of it. If we instead respond with love, or at least attempt to understand and not judge others, we create opportunities for peace. This will give us time to discover what we have in common with our new family members. In this and previous chapters, the focus has been on negotiating differences. In the next, we will look at the significance of shared values.

# *C h a p t e r  F o u r*

# *VALUES THAT KEEP US TOGETHER*

*It is possible to love someone* who has values completely different from your own, but differences in values are the greatest threat to a strong relationship. Let's say you're married to someone who places financial wealth and excitement at the top of his list of what's most important in life, while, above all, you value family and tranquility. You can imagine why the two of you would often be at odds.

As important as shared values might be to a couple, in some multicultural unions, we can get so caught up in noticing differences that we forget to consider whether or not we agree with our partners on what matters most. So if you're in a relationship for the long run, ask yourself this question: If my mate and I were roused in the middle of the night, our home going up in flames, what one thing would each of us reach for?

Our family was forced to consider this question when we lived in Northern California. Mark was out of town on business, when the children and I learned that a wind-driven inferno was heading toward our neighborhood. I'd spent years writing a novel under contract with a New York publisher, but I didn't reach for my computer disks. My first thought was for a copy of a book my mother had written when I was in the third grade. I had been so proud when I introduced my mom and her book to the class. On the day of the fire, her book was the one object I raced to collect.

"I've got something for Dad, so let's get out of here," our oldest son, H. P., called. He and the younger children, Carolyn and Mark Jr., and I rushed to the car. After driving a safe distance, I glanced down to see what H. P. felt was Mark's most treasured possession. It was a worn out, circa 1950, dime store copy of *Pinocchio*. Mark had shared with us memories of snuggling beside his mom as she lovingly read it. Consider our choices: books and family and love. They say nothing about race, but speak volumes about the values that hold us together.

He has been married twice and was known as a relentless wom-
anizer, but movie idol Clint Eastwood gave up his freedom for
marriage to a woman with whom he shops for groceries at
Safeway. Together they visit her mom, who works at Montgom-
ery Ward. Since 1994, Eastwood has been married to the former
Dina Ruiz, who is a blend of Anglo, Asian, and black. They met
when she was an anchor for a small Northern California television station. Eastwood is now seventy and his bride thirty-
four. They have a three-year-old daughter and are said to be
blissfully happy.[9]

Why would a Hollywood legend choose reality, when fantasy
is so alluring? The truth is, no matter how high we may go in
life, we remain at the core our true selves. Eastwood may have
realized that finding the right partner has little to do with exterior differences, but that it does have a great deal to do with
finding someone who shares your values.

Anne Goodoff, a midwestern socialite of Scottish, English,
and Irish ancestry, whose forebears arrived in America in the
early 1700s, would agree that a marriage in which two people
have opposing values is not much of a marriage at all. Raised in
a tony St. Louis suburb, in 1980, Anne married a man who

seemed to be the perfect match: they had been raised only miles apart, had similar family trees, and shared memories of summers at local country clubs.

But once they married, she and her husband, Edward, seemed to move in different directions. He built a Fortune-500 firm, and was often away on business seven days a week, including major holidays. She was occupied with volunteer work, raising their three children, and trying to keep them grounded, despite their wealth. "When Edward was home he wouldn't have been caught dead doing something family oriented, like sitting down and playing a board game," she said. When Edward resisted changing his hectic lifestyle, Anne ended their decade-long marriage with a divorce.

She has since remarried a man with a background quite different from her own. Leo Manetta, Chicago born, is an Italian American whose ancestors arrived in the U.S. two generations ago. The son of a baseball coach, Leo heads a midwestern school system.

Cultural differences aside, Anne thinks she couldn't have found a better match. "Leo's life is centered on how much time he can spend with the kids and me. I never feel that anything else ever comes before us." In addition to her three children from her first marriage, Anne and Leo are now the parents of a three-year-old girl. The six of them spend time together. They have visited Disney World, traveled to Aruba to see a solar eclipse, and even find time for board games. Sundays they attend a local church.

When Anne discussed the impact of her divorce on her three oldest children, she said she is convinced that it was the best change she could have made in their lives. She didn't want them growing up thinking the empty marriage they witnessed in that big house on the lake was really a marriage. Anne said, "All that money, that power, that wasn't me. It didn't make me feel any better. What's most important is that the person you spend your life with is someone with whom you can have a shared life. When you have the same values, you want the same things." Her ex-husband, by the way, has also remarried, to a woman who shares his values: she has an all-consuming interest in the business world.

Back in 1963, college students Jenny and Ted Peters, who are both European American, were drawn together by the same ideals. Both had been raised in predominantly white, middle-class neighborhoods (she in Ohio, he in Michigan), but as they rubbed shoulders with college students of different races, they vowed to never again live in a homogeneous world. Jenny was also further affected by a choir tour through Asia. "I saw people experiencing real poverty. You see it on the news, but the reality is much harsher. The refugee areas made a big impact on me. I thought every little thing we have [in the United States] is so much more than these people have."

Married in 1964, both Jenny and Ted became educators. After the 1969 birth of their son, Paul, they applied to become adoptive parents. Before long their family had added Kathy Kim, an infant from Korea, and Elizabeth, who is Pakistani and Portuguese.

But they didn't stop there. Over the years, the couple has also taken in a number of exchange students, including Zulu brothers from South Africa. Ted had been their father's teacher. When the parents went back home, the Peters helped raise money among their friends to defray college tuition costs for the young men. Jenny once took the brothers to buy new jackets, and a salesclerk, noticing how close the three were, asked one of them if Jenny was their mother. He said, "She's my American mom." His answer was a reminder that working in tandem, Jenny and Ted followed through on ideals born more than three decades earlier.

Among many of the couples I interviewed, when it came to values, getting good educations for their children was at the top of their lists. Peter, the Irish American who is a chemist, wanted to create a home where there was a great interest in learning.

This had not been a priority in his childhood home. In fact, he said his family considered him weird because he liked books.

His wife Linda's experiences stand in contrast. Raised in a Chinese-American family, she was taught that life was about school and learning. "Education was highly stressed in my family," she said. "You had to have an 'A'. I'd give my dad my report card and he would look to see if there was anything below an 'A'. Nothing else was acceptable." Linda said she was so busy with school, piano lessons, and two-hour-a-day, six-day-a-week Chinese school, that she never had time for play or for after-school activities.

She believes this quest for excellence was her family's bid for respect. Not going to college would have been unthinkable. "My father felt that only one school was acceptable, U. C. Berkeley. When I wanted to apply to Smith, he said, 'What on earth is this? Why would you want that?' For him, there was only one profession to aim for, doctor. You become an M.D. because a doctor gets accepted, gets respect, gets included in American society. Should you choose anything else, the job can't be labor intensive or menial." She said her dad was so determined to "influence" his daughters' careers that he filled out Linda's pharmacy school applications and helped write some of her sister's college reports.

When they were sharing childhood stories and Linda heard that Peter's parents had a laissez-faire attitude about his education, she said, "You mean your parents told you to just go out and play?" Now that they have children, ten and eight years old, Linda and Peter have created a happy mix of both their backgrounds. Rather than the less-challenging local school, their children are enrolled in a more demanding parochial school. They're enrolled in Chinese school, but on weekends only. That leaves them time for something Linda considers as essential as homework—play.

Most people are like Peter and Linda, longing for what they don't have. Ritchie, who is a European American from a well-to-do family, wishes she'd had what her husband, Bob, a Lakota Indian, had in abundance, a strong and close family.

Bob lived in a working-class subdivision, but his family must have seemed wealthy compared to their families on the reservation, whom they visited every weekend. "At my maternal uncle's house there was no running water or indoor plumbing. They used wood to heat the house. But they seemed happy," said Bob.

He also recalled his paternal grandfather taking the family to pow-wows, when Lakota tribes gathered: "There were traditional foods, deer-meat soup, tripe, and fry bread. My parents had a green army canvas tent. There would be five of us kids and our family dog. I remember laying there during one pow-wow. The drumming and dancing continued all night, and I could feel the drum beat through the ground and hear people laughing and exchanging greetings. I look back and feel peaceful and comfortable, just remembering."

There are many stories that convey the values in Bob's family. Two involve Bob's father, who, in the eighth grade, was forced to attend a government boarding school, where children were punished for speaking their native languages or practicing their tribal customs. Missing his family, Bob's father, a cousin, and a friend, escaped. They knew getting free was a long shot. It was a fifty-mile trip home, and school authorities were known for tracking down runaways. Bob's dad and the other boys took off running, and when they looked back, they saw one of their teachers in a Model-T, with the school's fastest runners standing on the sideboards. Catching them was just sport for those boys. For Bob's father, escaping meant returning home and being with the family he loved. Bob's dad and his companions sped up and outdistanced the car. When he reached home, Bob's dad told his parents he wanted to remain home, and they found him a job as a cowboy.

He continued in this line of work until he was eighteen, when he enlisted to fight in the Korean war. "Military service was considered honorable, an idea that stems from the warrior tradition," Bob said. His father didn't contact the family for a year, which was unusual. During his Christmas leave, he returned laden with gifts, but kept his homecoming a secret. "When his cab pulled up and word got around that he was back, his brothers and sisters and aunts and uncles, cousins, and friends came spilling out in the snow, welcoming him back."

Hearing these stories, and then experiencing the family up close, convinced Ritchie that she needed that kind of closeness. "The first time I met Bob's family and saw everyone together, I felt that they had a strong sense of being connected to one another. They displayed more of an unconditional love. In my family it was clear: 'We love you, but we won't if you cross the line.' I had a huge grief reaction watching Bob with his family. It was something I'd always wanted for myself."

That's what they have created together. Bob is now a graduate student and Ritchie works part-time at a bookstore. The family often visits a New York City playground, where I observed them. Seated on a bench, Bob cradled his baby daughter, Reed, five months old. Nearby, Grant, their three-year-old, was just recovering from a spill and was being comforted by Mom. Perhaps Grant and Reed will one day share with others their memories of a rich family life.

Janna and Donald (who are African American and German-Swedish American, respectively) have also created a family life that reflects their values of love, spirituality, and intellectual enrichment. But if we had been flies on the wall the first night they spent time together in 1978, we certainly wouldn't have guessed the two had anything in common. They met at Indiana University, when Donald was a senior and chairperson of the orientation committee, and Janna was a first-year grad student and a dormitory residence assistant.

While they were both brought up in Indiana, their lives were quite different. She is the daughter of conservative Baptists. Her dad was a teacher and her mother, a registered nurse. In this African-American household, there was no card playing because it was considered "the work of the devil." There was no drinking either, except occasionally by her father, at which times he was severely admonished by her mother. Janna, who was discouraged from dating, wasn't a party girl anyway. "In high school, I had a friend take me to the senior prom and we were home by 10:30." She preferred books, and spent years honing her intellectual skills, eventually earning a Ph.D. in English.

Donald's home was more conventional. His father was a construction supervisor and his mom, a homemaker. "I suspect my paternal grandparents were Jewish," Donald said. If so, they made every effort to conceal it. On his mother's side, they were Swedish immigrants. "It was the classic Ellis Island experience," he said. As a handsome and charming achiever, Donald fit right in with the university's predominantly white population. He grew somewhat jaded, and admitted he was an intellectual snob. "I didn't believe in love." For him, love was one more subject to debate and skewer.

In his senior year, he lived with a girlfriend in an off-campus apartment, and was about to throw a party for other student staff members, when, to be polite, he invited Janna. Once the party got going, it was wild, reflecting the hedonism of the seventies. "Folks were smoking, drinking, the works. Then I heard a knock at the door. Understand that no one knocked on campus doors in the seventies. I thought it was the police. When I opened the door, there were three things I noticed about Janna: First, this was the era of hippiedom, but she was holding a purse—I hadn't seen a girl carry one in four years. Second, she was wearing a dress, something else I hadn't seen. And third, Janna's wearing these neat little bangs. She sits down and crosses her legs, looking all around her at this wild scene."

Janna said she was thinking, "If this is the staff, what in the world are the students going to be like?"

Donald offered her a drink. She said, "I don't drink."

Donald was thinking, "She won't last a week on this campus."

Days passed before they ran into one another again. "Completely on a lark, with no hidden agenda," said Donald, "I invited her to have a cup of coffee."

Janna recalled accepting his invitation out of loneliness. "I had noticed Donald and thought that at least he was kind, though I disapproved that he was living [out of wedlock] with a woman."

They both said at the same time, "We went to the Runcible Spoon Coffee House." Donald continued, "and we began talking." Hours later, he was so impressed with her that he knew he was falling in love. "She's so smart, had such interesting things to say. I was completely taken. I knew this was the person I had to marry."

The next year Donald left for graduate school in Ohio, but they continued to correspond. Believing their common intellectual interests could serve as a vital bond, he was determined that he had to have this woman. But after he proposed, Janna wrote him a disappointing letter, listing fifty reasons why they shouldn't marry, many of those reasons having to do with race. She had written, "If you take on a black wife, you will change the composite of your whole social status—it will be lowered in the eyes of others. We'll lose jobs or job opportunities."

Janna said, "I didn't want him to look at me one day and say 'Because of you I wasn't able to ...'"

Determined not to let her go, Donald answered her with a list of one hundred reasons why they should be together. He convinced her. They did marry. In their lives together, they have enjoyed financial and spiritual prosperity, and live in luxury. All of this has given Donald the opportunity to prove her wrong. He said of their lives, "I fell dramatically and completely in love with Janna, and it is absolutely the best thing that's ever happened to me." Twenty years into their marriage, this is indeed high praise.

I was often taken aback and touched during interviews, when husbands, like Donald, made the most romantic declarations about their wives. One man told me that his wife made life worth living, while another penned poetry—and this from couples who had been working out differences for as long as fifty years. My husband is more typical when it comes to declarations of love, you know, the glowing messages in Valentine's and anniversary cards.

I have to admit, though, that I once tried to change him. It all started one night when Mark was working on some notes, and I wanted his attention. I said, "You know, one of the things I miss about being around African-American men is that they really know how to rap to their women."

Lest you think I was asking him to sing for me, you should know that before the rise of hip-hop, "rap" was a word used to describe the heights of rapture that black men could send their women into by stylistically weaving their words together. With rhythmic cadences, these compliments are an outgrowth of the African oral tradition. Held captive in America, our men had nothing to offer their lovers, not even the promise of tomorrow, but at least they could offer endearing utterances.

Hearing of this history, Mark tried to rise to the challenge, and suggested I give him a clue about what to say. Starting with something easy, I pointed to one of my legs. "Some brothers compliment womens' legs by calling them 'bad,' which means 'fine.' Wag your head a bit and say, 'You got some bad legs, Mama.' Clearly enjoying the moment, Mark bobbed his head, saying in a monotone, 'Mother, you have very bad legs.'

We were convulsed in giggles, and then, with Mark's black-in-training course ended, he led me toward his computer, promising to compose an on-the-spot message. He appeared deep in thought, then, as he began to type, these words appeared on screen: "I so love hearing you speak, I could eat the words that come from your mouth." This is one of my favorite memories of my beloved husband, a reminder to concentrate on that which is of greatest importance to us—intangibles that can sustain us through difficult times.

##  THAT FIGHTING SPIRIT

Another value that draws individuals together can be their fighting spirits, their ability to look adversity in the face and wrestle it to the ground. That was one of the traits television talk show host Montel Williams, who is African American, saw in his European-American wife, Grace, a former Las Vegas showgirl and actress. They met during the taping of his show, have been married for seven years, and now have two children.

That they are both fighters may make all the difference in the quality of their lives, especially now that Montel, forty-three, has been diagnosed with multiple sclerosis, a debilitating neurological disease. According to *People* magazine, during a low point, Williams told Grace he expected she would want to leave him, now that he wasn't the man she had married. Grace, thirty-four, didn't go meekly into the night. Her response was, "Listen you selfish little bastard. Who do you think you are? There is a reason why you got this. The Man up there picked you for a reason, and you should count it as one of your blessings."[10]

Williams has credited his wife with giving him the strength to fight his disease. He participates in a medical regimen designed to slow the disease's progression, maintains a grueling workout schedule, and has raised more than $80,000 for MS research."

Williams and his wife make it sound as if two fighters are better than one. Nancy Katsura, an African American, and Kohei Katsura, who is Japanese, certainly found two to be a powerful sum. Married for thirteen years, they have long valued one another for their fighting spirits. One occasion in particular taught them that they can take turns bolstering one another.

It was two in the morning in their Tokyo home, when Nancy realized that Kohei was tormented about his business. "My husband is not what some people think of as the typical man. He does talk to me about everything, and for more than ten years I've listened to his concerns about his business. But on this particular night, there was something different about the way he sounded. He was upset about having to cut back his workforce and let some employees go. In Japan, many businesses are run like families, and the bosses really care about their employees and their dependents. Of course, any business-related setback is disappointing, but Kohei was just staring at the ceiling, apologizing for what he called 'letting me down.' I could feel his despair."

Nancy said that although the recession was cutting into many Japanese businesses, as was the case for Kohei, many of the men blame themselves. They believe they're bringing dishonor to their families, their nation, and even their deceased ancestors.

Nancy has a master's degree in social work, has been a Parisian model, and trained as an interior designer—work which has given her entrée to rarefied circles. She speaks French and Japanese, but the only language she spoke that night, as she fought for her husband's spirit, was the vernacular she had learned growing up. Sitting upright, she shouted, "Don't even go there!"

Nancy continued to talk and listen, turning the conversation from despair to hope. She told Kohei, "We pay homage to your dead ancestors, and we can honor mine too. They also have something to offer. Black people have been forced to learn how to survive. I'm filled with their strengths and can share them with you. Whatever happens, we get through this together and we *do* get through it."

Looking back, Nancy felt her "little sermon" marked a turning point. Before the night was over, they laughed and hugged. Less than a year later, her husband's business began to turn around. That was four years ago. Today his business, Director's

Studio, is thriving. New accounts have taken them throughout Western Europe, Hong Kong, the People's Republic of China, and Egypt, as they produce and direct haute couture fashion shows and other exhibitions. Kohei feels that with Nancy at his side, they can accomplish anything.

Because they're forced to stand up to ignorance, many multicultural couples value that fighting spirit in one another. But when they aren't using that fighting spirit against their adversaries, and instead against their lovers, they can either mow the other person down or hope that their partners are equally as strong.

Evelyn must have sensed that marriage with a pushover wouldn't last, and she would have had good reason for believing so. On one side of her family, her ancestors were Puritans who braved the voyage to America in the seventeenth century. On the other side, her ancestors were Italian immigrants who were also courageous enough to give up that which had been familiar to them to start a new life in America. Extremely bright, Evelyn can be counted on to speak her mind.

Her husband, James, every bit her intellectual match, said they have "ethnically stereotypical temperament differences." She described him as "stoic, much less verbal, and stubborn," and she characterized herself as "verbal about most things (good and bad), stubborn, hotter-tempered, and Mediterranean." You'll note that they have stubbornness in common. James said, "There are times when Evelyn wants to bargain toward a solution, while I just want to find the optimal solution." She added, "He's wrong."

Some who know them would describe him as the more "laid-back" of the two, but somehow you just know they couldn't have maintained their twenty-two year marriage if they had not been equally strong. Evelyn said it's important that young people understand that "when two people get married, they are also marrying each other's families." She was referring to obligations, but might have also been alluding to inherited traits, because like her, James got his strong backbone from his parents.

During the 1930s, James's parents were administrators for a Japanese orphanage in Los Angeles. They became engaged before World War II and moved up their wedding date when they learned they would be forced into the Japanese internment program in 1942 and that they would be housed with their immediate family members. In this shameful period of America's history, Japanese Americans, many highly patriotic, hard-working individuals, were detained by the War Relocation Authority because the United States government suspected they would be traitorous. Families were uprooted as they were forced to evacuate and were transported to concentration-style camps. Educations and careers were cut short, friendships terminated, lovers separated, and homes destroyed by looting and conflagrations. Children weren't given any special considerations.

James's parents learned that government administrators planned to take the seventy-five children in their orphanage, as well as another group from San Francisco, and separate them from their longtime caretakers. Understandably, James's parents opposed this scheme because the children had bonded with their caretakers. Another loss could be severely detrimental to them. James's parents stood up to authorities, insisting the government build an orphanage for the children within an internment camp, where they could have the same caretakers. Their plans were followed, and buildings were constructed in Manzanar, California. Further, they were given a cook with a separate kitchen, and bathrooms—all-around better facilities. Most importantly, the children were not abandoned by the adults they trusted.

James's father wasn't through though. When construction was complete, buses were provided to transport the children to Manzanar, but no one had considered how their cribs would be conveyed. James said, "By a certain day, everyone who was Japanese had left the city of Los Angeles, except my father. He remained behind, insisting the cribs be transported so the younger children could sleep in their familiar beds." There was something about his father's quiet determination that made it difficult to say no. That night, the children slept in their own beds.

With their individual family histories, it's not surprising that James and Evelyn admit they're stubborn. But their union is a model for how a couple can use their strengths to bolster rather than destroy one another. James said, "After going through a litany of differences, we need to get down to the bottom line— the fact that we have been married for twenty-two years and still love each other." Evelyn added, "What has made that possible is patience, hard work, and the ability to compromise, eventually. I can't overestimate the need for hard work to make any long-term relationship work."

Sometimes an individual is attracted to a partner who has the inner strength that Evelyn and James exemplify, but she may not realize that she's just as strong. Such was the case with Kelly, now forty-nine, who is an Irish Catholic raised in Milwaukee, and David, now forty-seven, who was raised in New York by non-practicing Jews who were atheists.

Kelly's and David's childhoods couldn't have been more unalike. She and her siblings went to mass seven days a week, and didn't dare complain about it. "We could not voice criticisms about the church and were not allowed to argue with our parents. When we had guests at the house, we kids weren't allowed to talk."

Despite their traditional lifestyle, it was always expected that Kelly would go to college. Her mother told her, "Don't let anyone tell you you can't do something because you're a woman." With hard work, Kelly won a scholarship to Harvard. She recalled, "I was seventeen and so happy to go. My home situation was suffocating."

At school, she wore the colorful styles of the seventies. When she went home, "I'd dress in whatever clothes I figured my parents wanted me to." For five years, Kelly lived with her boyfriend but didn't tell her parents. "I knew they would have a fit. I felt I was leading a double life."

Just a few years behind Kelly, on New York's Upper West Side, David was starting life with his unconventional mother and maternal grandfather. "One of my earliest memories is standing between my grandfather's legs, arguing with a neighbor, an Orthodox Jew, that there was no God. My grandfather had said he would want to disown me if I became religious. I was in the first grade, and I can still feel his hand on my shoulder, as if saying 'good boy.'"

David hails from a long line of iconoclasts: At nineteen, his maternal great-grandfather avoided conscription in the Czarist army by fleeing to the United States, where he met his future partner, who was also Russian. They eventually had David's grandfather, a man who would one day flee the U.S. for Canada to avoid the World War II draft. After returning to the States, he began living with David's grandmother. They shunned marriage.

With his dark hair and pale skin, David resembles his Russian ancestors. But when David was eight, his mother explained that his father was an African-American man she had known. David met his father when he was sixteen, but they have otherwise had no contact. David said of his racial identity, "I've never thought of myself as being black or white or other. When I was a boy, my mother said I was a combination of all the races and all the people of the world. I never had a distinct racial identity, but my identity is more white than black." For many years, David and his mother lived with her husband, a European-American physician who was involved in social causes.

Growing up surrounded by gays and lesbians, African Americans, Caucasians, West Indians, Cubans, and Puerto Ricans, as well as artists and musicians, David said, "I didn't understand as a child and emotionally do not understand now, the social and cultural distinctions people make. My experience was that a man or a woman had value or they didn't."

From the beginning, David challenged authority. In the second grade, he called his teacher a liar. "When he manhandled me, I reported him to the principal," he recalled. By high school he was involved in anti-Vietnam protests and got the ROTC kicked off of campus. All of this was championed by his mother.

His successes led him to run on a peace ticket for student body president. Much to the chagrin of administrators, he won. Several protests later, school officials scheduled impeachment proceedings against him, and David lost his presidency by one vote. Transferring to a private boarding school, he discovered administrators there didn't like him any better, and he was eventually thrown out on charges of drug possession. He called it a setup. "They accused me on the only night in the school year when my friends and I weren't using drugs."

Finally, his mother was fed up with his school troubles, but she and his stepfather helped him to elude arrest. With the engine running and his bags hastily thrown in the back of the car, they spirited David away. In the stretches between completing high school and college, he repeated a pattern of enrolling and being thrown out, interspersed with travel throughout Europe and North Africa. This pattern ended when

David realized he could put his fighting spirit to work and get paid for it—he could become a lawyer.

He met Kelly at law school in the summer of 1976. David said, "I was walking down the hall, and I remember seeing a woman with long red hair and a shapely figure and I remember following her." That was the start of their relationship. Kelly had taken a circuitous route away from the status quo, growing more leftist as she worked, counseling girls in a halfway house and then in a law library, as she considered becoming a barrister.

From the beginning, Kelly and David agreed they didn't want a serious relationship. No commitments, just lots of fun. She found in David the adventurous, free-wheeling side of herself she'd kept closeted from her conservative parents. She wouldn't be in hiding much longer. A few years into their relationship, just as Kelly was starting her first year of law school, she called David to say, "I'm pregnant. Are you going to leave me?"

He did what his grandfather and his grandfather before him had done: he invited her to share his life with him, for the meantime, anyway. Kelly said, "I was thrilled, madly in love but terrified of my parents. Here I was at twenty-eight. I'd put myself through college and started law school, and I'd been supporting myself for ten years, but it took me two weeks to build up the courage to phone my parents. That phone call was one of the hardest things I'd done."

Her mother said, "I always knew you'd get yourself in a mess."

Not surprisingly, David's mother had a different reaction. "She threw us a party and invited everybody we knew," said David. When Kelly's father asked David about his intentions concerning his daughter, David explained that he was a traditionalist. "I told him that my maternal grandfather didn't marry my grandmother, my mother didn't marry my father, that what was good enough for them is good enough for me."

Both attorneys, David and Kelly have been together for nineteen years. David said, "My life with Kelly is about as perfect as it could be. I enjoy her mind. I enjoy being with her. We have fun with each other. I like her. I respect much of what she does. One of the things we want to maintain is a level of independence that allows us to be our own people and to be together. I could not live with a person who is on my neck. I need the ability to feel I can float away with the understanding that I will always return. Ours is a good fit and always has been."

Her parents continue to worry about Kelly and David living together unmarried, but they are pleased with their three grandchildren, who have been raised, by the way, much like

David, surrounded by people of many backgrounds. Their first baby-sitters, in fact, were a gay couple, one African-American, the other European-American. Said David, "They were the only people we trusted our son with."

Kelly suspects that, as adults, their children will "rebel" from their parents' way of life and marry. David also believes they will look back in gratitude at their lives. "In their experience, a lot of their friends come from divorced homes. We happen to be one of the more stable relationships in their world."

David has served somewhat as a liberating force on Kelly's life. Every once in a while though, Kelly said, when she's talking to David or her kids, "rigid Catholic school—inspired words will pop out of my mouth, and I know that's my past rearing its head." She had long stopped attending religious services before she met David, and said she has no ties to the church. But she lobbies for a Christmas tree. They compromise, getting one every other year.

Kelly said, "Too many couples feel they have to sit down and confront every issue, with the focus on changing the other person. I say don't let it annoy you, but it will if you give it too much energy. You have to figure out what matters and what doesn't. If you really love that person, give him the benefit of the doubt. Your level of trust should be high."

David concluded, "Just let the issue go. That's much more important than acclamations of love."

David and Kelly didn't have to negotiate religious differences, as quite a few multicultural couples must. Among the people I interviewed, those who are involved in an active and mutual spiritual life felt their faith was one of the most important aspects of their lives together. According to one study, "The greatest predictor of marital stability for all couples was that they participated in shared religious activities and had fewer religious differences."[12]

## ʃᐯᐯᐧ *UNITED BY ONE SPIRIT* ʃᐯᐯᐧ

Among the couples I interviewed who are religious, only two recent college graduates who were dating were convinced that their religious differences didn't matter. But of course they matter, and increasingly so when there are children in the picture. What's important is how couples negotiate their differences. Although I read studies that suggest religious differences can destroy marriages, among the people I interviewed, all of them had worked out many of the conflicts that existed. Certainly one explanation for this is that as couples who have built long-term marriages, they put a lot of effort into communicating and negotiating with one another.

The couples used one of four approaches: they renounced their faith or participated in religious services only during holidays; one partner converted to the other partner's faith; they found another religion or denomination that was mutually satisfying; or each partner maintained separate religious practices, and in some of these cases, they took turns attending one another's services.

When they first married, Evelyn and James were not members of a church. Evelyn, of Italian American and WASP origins, said of her religious upbringing, "I'm from a Puritan, dour Presbyterian background. In my childhood church, there was hellfire and brimstone from the pulpit. If you were enjoying yourself, it must be a sin. And *don't* believe what it says in the Bible; you're *never* forgiven for anything." As a teenager, she stopped going to church, and as it turned out, so had her future husband, a Japanese American who was raised as an Episcopalian.

When they were expecting a child, however, Evelyn and James wanted to bring their daughter up with a rich spiritual life. They instinctively knew that although Evelyn's family's style of Presbyterianism worked for some, it was not for a child they wanted to raise. They eventually had their daughter christened in an Episcopal parish that could offer something more than guilt-inducing sermons. Evelyn has embraced Episcopal traditions. She said, "Considering my church history, the concept of confession and absolution every Sunday is nothing short of a miracle from God."

That she gained an appreciation for another tradition that led her ultimately to discover new insights in her childhood faith, underscores one of the most significant themes in interreligious dialogue. By becoming familiar with another tradition, we can go back and truly appreciate aspects of our own traditions in ways we had not seen before. Elaine Tokunaga, a Scottish American and the granddaughter of Methodist ministers, would agree.

Although separated from her husband, who is Japanese American, Elaine said her religious life was phenomenally enriched by his Buddhist traditions. A member of the Dutch Reformed Church, she said, "Until the time I met my husband, I thought the world should be strictly Christian, and that there shouldn't be any deviation. But when he explained Buddhism, that opened me up to different possibilities, and to a perspective that all religions are one. At the center of religious life, there is a common goodness."

Elizabeth, thirty-seven, a college English teacher, has created a life based on this principle of common goodness within different religions. She is Christian and her husband, Michael, is Jewish. The couple attends a synagogue together twice a month. Elizabeth attends a Protestant church two times a month, with Michael accompanying her once a month. "We're in love and love to be together," she said. "We also believe in the same God. God gave me to Michael, and Michael to me," said Elizabeth. "To worship separately would be wrong. I love Jewish liturgy. I have these fond feelings of continuity and associate certain prayers with high holy days. After all, Jesus was a Jew." On Fridays, she prepares Shabbat dinners for them, sometimes humming Baptist hymns as she works. Saturday mornings they read the Torah together.

Though a faithful adherent to Christianity, Elizabeth has long held an interest in Judaism. Her curiosity was sparked by a long-ago conversation. "My dad shared with me his childhood memories of visiting a synagogue and seeing the beautiful Torah and scrolls." Elizabeth's father also told her how, upon learning the extent of Holocaust crimes and the persecution of the Jews, he felt personal shame as an American. "He felt strongly that Americans should have known more, done more." What had been guilt for the father transformed into a hunger for understanding in the daughter. Elizabeth began to read books on Jewish history and did research on well-known Jewish people.

Some part of Elizabeth grew determined to incorporate both Judaism and Christianity into the daily course of her life. That silent aspiration grew after she fell in love with Michael, who is four years her junior. Introduced by mutual friends in 1993, among many mutual interests, their spirituality was particularly significant. Agreeing that neither should have to sacrifice cherished traditions, they were married by a rabbi under the traditional chuppa, the Jewish wedding canopy; theirs was made of Elizabeth's great-grandmother's lace tablecloth. They planned the ceremony carefully, discussing whether Michael would be comfortable with the inclusion of the words "Jesus Christ" in their prayers. Michael told her, "That's a part of what you're bringing to the marriage. We have the same God and you love me through Jesus."

Later, their baby daughter, Esther, was baptized as a Christian and was the guest of honor at her own Hebrew naming ceremony. Just outside the door jamb, as guests arrived at Elizabeth and Michael's home, they could see a mezzuzah, the encased scroll that is a sign and reminder of the Jewish faith. It is in keeping with the scripture that reads: "You shall tell the world our God is one God." In a sense, they have dedicated their union to this.

Some religious experts suggest that dual-faith couples like Elizabeth and Michael are doing a disservice to their children, because, while they'll grow up tolerant of both faiths, they will not develop their own deeply religious traditions. Others argue that choosing one religion for a child, when parents are of different faiths, sends the wrong message: if one parent renounces his or her religion, it must not be important. When the child is asked to choose, they say, the child can feel disloyal to one parent.

Fortunately for Paul, fifty-one, an engineer, none of these complications occurred in his home. His parents met as college students when they attended a Baptist adult school. Paul's father was actually the teacher. After their marriage, and the birth of two children, they continued to be active in their church. But when Paul was twelve, his mother became critical of Christianity. Paul said, "I remember a large discussion between my parents. My mother felt that mainstream churches had taken on an importance larger than God. She became critical of Christianity for a lack of relevance and a lack of vision. There were no heated arguments, not that I could see anyway, but my parents had a major conflict about this. Dad was an elder at our church, and a tenor in the choir."

Turning her back on doctrine-oriented religions, Paul's mother found spiritual freedom in Eastern and Near Eastern mystical traditions. How did his parents handle their differences? They seemed to agree to disagree, and they didn't involve their children in their conflict.

Paul said, "My relationship with my father continued as before. We worked side by side, but on the whole we stayed away from the subject of religion. My mother and I would talk unceasingly about things religious and philosophical." She didn't invite her husband into these conversations, and he didn't feel the need to jump in. As a result, Paul said, "There was never a time when I didn't feel close to both of them."

Perhaps because his mother's new interests never became a subject of rancor between her and her husband, she didn't feel locked into any one position. About fifteen years ago, Paul's mother converted back to Christianity. She was able to incorporate what she had learned during her exploratory phase into her long-cherished beliefs. More than thirty-five years later, Paul's parents are still close to one another.

What about Paul? Today, he and his wife are active in the

Baptist church. His oldest daughter, Stephanie, twenty-seven, describes him as a gifted parent, and this, she believes, is partially attributable to his deeply held faith. "It makes him very compassionate and a really good listener," she said. "I remember being young and having experienced some incident at school, someone making a nasty comment, something that made me feel icky. He was never surprised but was always well equipped to deal with it. He'd say 'Yes, this is part of your challenge, learning to understand it.' I think he learned to really think things out, then step back and ask, 'What do I need to do here?'"

Paul inherited from both of his parents a respect for religious observation and practice. But can religious traditions be passed on in families even when people believe they are not adherents to that particular faith? Opal, thirty-one, an artist, was surprised at how deeply rooted her traditions were, when she gave birth to her son a decade ago in Chattanooga, Tennessee. Like her parents, she is "culturally" Jewish, and she described herself as "highly spiritual," but she added, "I don't lead a religious life."

She and her husband, who is Christian, were asked to decide on whether or not their son would be circumcised. "Once he was in my arms, the urge to protect him was so primal," she said. But she was torn when the doctor pointed out that there was a synagogue nearby, and asked her if she wanted him to get the rabbi for a prayer and a *bris*.

A "bris" is a Jewish ceremony in which an infant boy is circumcised. Opal said, "In ancient times, circumcision was how you could tell a boy was Jewish." This was an aspect of herself she'd assumed she had never developed, but she found herself sobbing over her conflict. "I wondered how I could voluntarily decide to have something so painful performed on my son. Yet at the same time, there was this sensation that I would be doing something wrong not to have him circumcised." In the end, she and her husband decided to go ahead with the procedure.

Above and beyond their decision, though, their story offers a powerful message. We can be deeply affected by our familial traditions, and life-changing events can put us in touch with needs and emotions of which we were previously unaware. When couples have religious differences, what seems to work best is an agreement to remain open to and supportive of one another's changing needs.

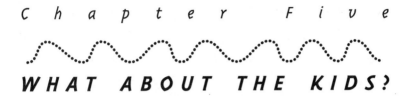

# WHAT ABOUT THE KIDS?

*There's a story that I heard* about a multicultural child. It seems the parents of a five-year-old had a new baby, and when they brought her home, big brother insisted on time alone with her. They tried stalling, for his parents worried about the baby's safety. He persisted. Then they finally hit upon a solution. "You can be alone with her," they said, and ushered their son into the nursery and left—leaving the door open just a crack to listen in.

Their boy did as instructed, no lifting his little sister, just standing and talking. It turned out he was concerned. The boy said to the baby, "They say I'm made in God's image. But can you tell me what God looks like? It has been so long since I was up there, I can't remember anymore."

The story is a reminder of what multicultural life is like from the perspective of children. In a world in which image and uniformity counts for so much, even the youngest try to make sense of what it means be "different." Of course this book explores all sorts of familial differences. In my home, for instance, issues of race and color have predominated. If your issues are somewhat different, I think you can still benefit from hearing a bit of my story and the decisions we made for our children.

Life seemed uncomplicated with my oldest son, H. P., since we are both African American. But once I married Mark, H. P. essentially had two dads—Mark, with whom we lived, and his African-American dad, who lives in Ohio. Although of different races, both of H. P.'s "dads" were close in color, and caused H.P. some concern about his own identity. Holding his beige hand alongside Mark's larger one, and noting they were nearly the same shade, little H. P. asked, "What color am I?"

I explained that he is black, a term that applies to race, even though it doesn't match his skin color, and he eventually accepted that. A few years later, when our middle child, Carolyn, with silky curls and olive skin, asked the same question, at the age of six, I had to bite my tongue. My first instinct was to use the old fearful message: "You're black and if you ever say anything different, people will quickly set you straight." By now I knew better. The fact that I felt as if I were choosing between my daughter's life and that of my people, however, is an indication of the deeply embedded sense of cultural loyalty that I and others feel.

Fortunately, Easter was coming up, and we found a way to communicate Carolyn's heritage in a more affirming message. We bought a cuddly brown and white bunny, and explained that his beauty had a lot to do with him being partially brown, partially white, and a combination of both, just like Carolyn, we told her, and just like our family, we told her and H. P.

Shortly thereafter, Mark Jr. was born. One of our more sardonic friends looked at his blue eyes, straight sandy-colored hair, and milky skin and said, "The way you're going, if you have another kid, the next one will be an albino." We needed jokes, life was getting complicated.

The stares began early on. People seemed shocked to see a black woman nursing a "white" infant. Later, an Austrian woman who had asked if Mark Jr. was mine, stared in disbelief, and then made a gesture over her belly as if simulating a pregnant form, and asked, "You mean he's yours, *yours*?" [Did you give birth to him?]

Another incident helped me make an important decision about my attitude toward all of this. During a cocktail party at a friend's house, I left Mark Jr. sleeping in a crib in an adjoining room. I didn't hear him when he awoke, so was I talking with a group of people when I saw a European-American woman emerge from the nursery holding my son. She worked her way around the room, looking for his mother, but when she reached me and I told her Mark Jr. was mine, she laughed and kept going. I waited, determined to let the scene play itself out. I have to give it to her, she thought fast. When the hostess assured her Mark Jr. was mine, this woman crossed the room, handed my child over, and said, "He's so cute, I didn't want to give him back to you."

She had helped me realize something important: These incidents weren't going to end [and they haven't], but they are not our lives. Children don't grow up confused about their identity because other people are confused, but because they haven't been given a clear signal from their parents. I imagine one day, I'll hear one of our children saying, "Sure, when I was growing up, there was all kinds of confusion about who I am, but I wasn't confused."

You may remember Bob Two Bulls, a member of the Oglala Lakota tribe. He wasn't confused, either. His surname dates back several generations, and although not considered unusual in his home state of South Dakota, it doesn't easily roll off the tongues of people in New York, where he and his family have temporarily settled. He gets all kinds of juvenile responses to his name, but he would never consider calling himself anything but who he is. That pride may stem from the fact that when he was a kid, his parents used to insist that he and his brothers leave the predominantly white housing development where they lived to accompany them every weekend to visit family who remained on the reservation. They were away so often that Bob couldn't get involved in the weekend sports he very much wanted to be a part of. His parents felt it was more important for their children to establish a clear cultural connection. Admittedly, it was a hard choice, but many years later, Bob is grateful for his parents' firm stance.

I've heard similar stories, whether it was someone who had to attend Ukrainian after-school classes or weekend Japanese school. Parents are often forced to make difficult choices, but their children are later grateful for the connection. In the next chapter, I'll tell you more about practical solutions that Mark and I and other parents have devised to help multicultural children develop strong self-identities. But first, you'll want hear from those who are out there every day, experiencing the ups and downs of being multicultural offspring.

Among the experiences that cause the most discomfort for some multicultural families are the constant questions and stares. One little boy, Christopher, ten, is Irish and Chinese American, and resembles both his parents. Christopher and his eight-year-old sister attend a Catholic school and a weekend Chinese school. He said, "Some kids ask, 'Are you mixed?' Chinese kids say, 'You don't look Chinese.' White kids say, 'You look Chinese.' One guy bowed at me. I guess he thought I was Japanese. Why does everybody care?"

Perhaps because young children do tend to be more direct, questions about differences can easily be answered, and quite literally. Take the story of one little boy and his mommy. It was just before Christmas in Inge Richardson's home, where the large picture window provided a view of the new snow as Inge cut festive shapes from a cookie recipe she had learned growing up in Germany. The door to her son's room opened. Earl was six at the time, enjoying his first play date—one more American custom the foreign-born bride would have to familiarize herself with. Little Earl was studying her intently, and she knew a question was coming.

"Mommy?"

"Yes dear?" she said in her melodious accent.

"My friend says you talk funny. You don't do you, Mommy?"

"No, I don't," she replied.

Earl's friend had followed timidly from the room and now stood watching them, sucking his thumb. Sounding relieved, Earl told him, "See, I told you she doesn't talk funny." They both shrugged and returned to their play.

Inge had actually communicated to her son that when it comes to handling potential problems, attitude is everything. Adults aren't the only teachers though. We can learn from our children. That's what happened in the Peters family. Kathy Kim, then five years old, the adopted Korean-born daughter of Jenny and Ted Peters, both European Americans, had just moved with her parents to New Orleans, where her father was teaching at a local seminary. Mother and daughter took a trip to the lake. Excited about being there, Kathy Kim was running a few steps ahead on the narrow path, when a group of boys passed and laughed and pointed at her.

Noticing her daughter's sudden sadness, Jenny asked what the boys had said to her. Kathy Kim said, "Mommy, they weren't being very nice to me." Hot under the collar, Jenny turned to go back and confront the boys. But Kathy Kim restrained her, and said, "It's okay, Mommy. I forgive them." Kathy Kim's behavior can offer us a new twist on an old saying: Forgive them, for they may know what they do, but have never learned any better.

Another lesson our children can teach us is that love can't be rushed. When I get impatient about relationships not developing as quickly as I would like them to, I've learned to say, "It will happen in God's time." Unlike busy humans, God, who is love, doesn't live by watches—and neither do feelings.

Frances Caro-Capolungo, for example, was deeply in love with her new husband, Ralph, but she couldn't say the same for her son, Marcos, who at the time was seven. He missed his father, who had returned temporarily to Mexico after he and Frances divorced, and the boy took it out on Ralph by breaking his belongings and generally mistreating him. Ralph's response only made Frances admire him more; he remained persistent and loving. The thought did cross her mind that perhaps it was too much to expect that love could bridge the gap between a white man and a Mexican divorcée and her son.

Hoping to get through to her boy, Frances asked him to take a seat. "Marcos, this is going to have to stop." The boy hung his head, his eyelashes wet with tears. Frances sighed dramatically, "I guess I'm going to have to divorce Ralph."

Her son looked alarmed. "Why, Mommy?"

"He doesn't deserve this kind of treatment," she said.

"But Mommy, you don't understand.

"What, Marcos?"

"I love that man."

More than two decades have passed since that mother-and-son conversation. Ralph's hair is now white and Marcos is a man. Ralph says with a pleased smile. "Now he's my son."

Children grow older, of course, and more complicated. When the need to "be like everyone else" intensifies, they are buffeted by experiences both good and hurtful.

## WORKING THROUGH PREJUDICE

Jean-Paul, sixteen, used to wish he could attend the local public school with the other kids on his block, but his parents insisted that he remain in a French-American school so he could keep up his language skills. His mom, a European American, was born and raised in Texas. His father is from France. They have been returning to France each summer since Jean-Paul was an infant.

"I think because my dad is French, he has a different set of standards from most American parents. He's stricter. Every time I get a grade report he'll say something like, 'Good job, but you could do better.' If I'm not as polite as he thinks I should be, then he will openly correct me and make me reintroduce myself. My mom would let it slide and maybe slip in a comment later.

"I think the difference between French and American kids is more in what they like to do. My French friends are into mountaineering. They like to climb the Alps—there's a lot of outdoor activity. American kids like to watch a lot of T.V., play computer games, and Nintendo. My American friends see it as weird that my parents will let me drink wine. In France you're given a small glass, not enough to get drunk, but to appreciate the taste, to improve your appetite. A French kid who wants to get drunk would have to sneak it.

"As an adult, I would prefer to live in America. There's less unemployment and it's cheaper. When I have children, I'll raise them the way my parents raised me. Attending the French school was beneficial. Being able to speak two languages is a real advantage.

French kids look up to Americans. They'll say, 'You're from America? I wish I could go there too.' But at the same time, the French look down on Americans. We were with American friends in France and were speaking English. The waiters were speaking to one another in French, assuming we couldn't understand. They said, 'Those stupid tourists, what are they doing?' The waiters are more surly toward American tourists. They have a terrible attitude and give them the worst cuts of meat. They think Americans have lower standards. They mumble behind their backs, like 'stupid Americans.' When I start speaking to them in French, I get comments showing that they're surprised, like, 'Oh, you're American?'"

Like Jean-Paul, Rachel, seventeen, is also fluent in French. From an early age, she has been enrolled in a French language school because, in her Massachusetts neighborhood, it is the school with the most diverse student body. The daughter of a Polish-American mom and an African-American father, Rachel says her chocolate brown skin often leads people to make assumptions about who she should be. In high school, when she transferred to a boarding school, she became enmeshed in racial politics.

"In the cafeteria, I noticed a group of black kids who sit together," said Rachel. "They aren't racists. They have white friends but they feel they have to hang out together. I sit with my white roommate. Some of these black kids don't like me for that. One girl looked at my photo album and saw whites and Asians, and said, 'Where are the black people? Don't you have black friends?'"

Rachel is aware of laws created during slavery that dictated that if a person had "one drop of black blood" that person was black. She views the attitudes many people have today, that she must call herself black and not biracial, as a perpetuation of a system that should be dead and buried. Rachel said, "I refuse to get caught up in how other people want to label me. My sister is a few years older than I am, and she went through a difficult time. She wasn't considered 'black enough' by many of her peers. If they said, 'Oh, you live in a big house, you're too white,' she really took it to heart. My sister definitely came close to ruining her life. She had this fixed image that she had to hang out with the black kids who get in trouble, not the good black kids, and I think it messed her up. She got in a lot of fights.

"My best friend is black and white, another friend is Chinese and black, the other is Vietnamese and white. For a long time I dated a guy who is Chinese and white. My boyfriend is black. He once said, 'Sometimes you sound so white.' I told him 'There's no such thing as sounding white or black, but my mom is white, so of course I'm going to be like her in some ways. That's who I am.' I see myself as black and white; I'm not one or the other. Race has nothing to do with who you are or who your friends are.

"In elementary school a girl on the playground said I was ugly because I was black. I was very angry. When I was younger I wanted straight hair. I used to want to be white, like my mother. But I also once read a book about a black girl who had a black mother and father and she wanted to be white too. You grow out of that. And I've changed. I like who I am."

Can people "get over" issues as complicated as Rachel's story suggests, or do the issues persist and wear away at one's self-esteem? Gail Hewlett, who is Caucasian, believes you shouldn't want to "get over" the experiences, but should incorporate them into your life. She says that people often assume they should avoid conflict, but that conflict is actually an opportunity for growth. She should know. In the 1950s, when she was seven, her mother, an Irish-American divorcée, married an African-American man. Gail said, "He was the only father I knew."

The marriage lasted for eight years, long enough for strangers to call them "nigger lovers" and for a number of land-lords to refuse to rent to them. Looking back at that time, how-ever, Gail, now a photographic artist, said, "If someone says you shouldn't marry someone of another race because it will be so hard on the kids, that's just an excuse. Life is beautiful and it is what you make it." She views her mother's second marriage and her time with her African-American stepfather as a gift. As a result of her experiences, she said, "A person's color has never been an issue in my life." Since 1966, Gail has been married to Martinez Hewlett, a biologist from the University of Arizona.

Martinez, whose family is from Louisiana, is Creole, a blend of Native American, French, and African American. "I don't identify myself as black," he said. "The largest part of my heritage is Choctaw Indian. My grandfather came from Austria, and on my mother's side I have French ancestors. The African aspect of my history is lost. It may have been forgotten because people were embarrassed or it just wasn't recorded. My cultural reference has nothing to do with customs often associated with Southern blacks. But in my family, people have gone through wanting to be very black and being ashamed of being 'high yellow.' I think that has changed for the most part. Now they're saying, 'We really are Creole people and we have our own heritage.'"

Because some people view Martinez as African American, he and Gail have had some difficult experiences. "Race isn't an issue to me, but some people make it an issue, and they feel the need to decide who I am. Just when I think I've forgotten it, it gets slammed back at me. I actually came to the University of Arizona after I turned down an assistant professorship at the top school in my discipline. They wanted me because I was a minority. I accepted the position in Arizona because they hired me as a scientist. My wife and I have also had some bad incidents. She was even fired from a job, and we've had some doors slammed in our faces, but it didn't traumatize us."

Martinez believes that race is simply a label, that it's how people see themselves that is important. "Gail and I have a wonderful son. He's a naval pilot and he's a kick because he has blonde hair and looks prototypically Caucasian, but he isn't that way in his head. He loves to mess with people in the Navy. He tells them that he's black, but they don't believe him. They go, 'Yeah, bro.' Then he shows them paperwork that identifies him as black. When we come to visit, he takes me around and introduces me to his friends, and says 'Here's my dad,' and they say, 'Oh, he *is* black.' He loves it. He loves his family. He loves the whole mix.

"When he was younger he went to L. A. every summer to spend two weeks with my family. His best friends were African American. He never shied away from that aspect of himself. But he has learned to say 'I'm Irish and Creole. You either like it or you don't.' He married a Caucasian woman from Wyoming and her parents are among our best friends. We call them friends-in-law.

"My brother married a Filipino, one sister married a Mexican man, and the other sister married a Creole. We get together and have this very mixed family and all of these cultures are brought together. I think the media doesn't talk about those of us who are comfortable with being mixed because its not newsworthy."

Unlike the Hewletts, Ed Guerra, the owner of a small business, struggled with his cultural identity. He said his parents me. I'm wondering, what's wrong with this guy? He finally said, 'You have Jewish blood in you don't you?' I said, 'Why'd you ask?' He said, 'I could just tell, that's all.'

"To me there was no difference between me and the other kids in my neighborhood. I was Eddie who talked slang and went to the swimming pool. I remember this black girl calling me a white boy. When I said I wasn't white, she said, 'Yes, you are. You're not black, so you must be white.'

"Once when I tanned really dark, I was at Walgreen's with my mother. She was looking around for me but walked past me and I went, what is she looking for? She later told me, 'I was looking at you thinking, what a handsome little guy.' For a minute, my own mother didn't know who I was.

"The other day my cousin said, 'Do you remember when you used to wish you were black?' I guess I didn't want the struggle of not having a racial identity.

"In the sixth grade, we went on a field trip. We saw white suburban kids and what they lived like. I felt so different. I was in a state of shock. The facilities were so nice and there were so many wealthy white kids. It made me realize there was a whole 'nother world out there. It just looked so pleasurable and easy. I thought, why do these people live here and I live there?

"By the seventh grade I'd become hard and bitter, so filled

with hate I couldn't think straight, and I'd get called an Uncle Tom if I even talked to a white kid. We had to bring this white kid from church to our home. I didn't want it because I knew I would have to get in fights to protect him.

"I had been a good kid, but I became a thug. I got tired of getting beaten up. I became a member of a black gang. In the seventh grade, I started getting in gang fights, blacks against Filipino. Then sometimes the Filipinos would band with blacks against the Chinese. It's a sinful life. If I'd stayed with these guys any longer, I would have been robbing houses and sticking up people. The devil got hold of my mind. If someone stepped on my shoes, I'd say, 'You have to the count of three to wipe it off.' I'd fight white kids if they bumped into me. I was in fights and had seen guys pull out shotguns and swords. By the time I was fifteen I felt like a thirty-year-old. My friend's big brothers were pimps.

"There were times I wanted to pull out a gun and shoot myself in the head. I wanted to run through glass doors and bleed to death. I had a rifle and one night, I pointed it at my head. I was going to pull the trigger but for some reason, scripture came to my mind: Jesus is a friend that sticks closer than a brother.

"My mother wanted me to go to a religious crusade in Oakland. I said, 'I'll go if you promise me you won't ever talk to me about God again.' At the revival, the preacher read from Romans, 'For all who are led by the Spirit of God are the children of God.' I knew right then that the choice I was going to make was not to fight anymore, 'cause all I'd been fighting was myself. I went up on the stage. Keep in mind that I was a fellow who never cried, no matter how much my father beat me. But that night I cried. I asked God not to give up on me. I knew I could do right. I knew I'd never have to wonder again who I was. I am a child of God. Once I said that, a weight was lifted off me and I felt clean. My mind felt free."

Ed's story is clearly a reminder of the importance of parents talking to children about their cultural heritage and discussing the complicated subject of race. While no parent can completely shield a child from harm, a supportive family environment can make all the difference in the way young people view themselves.

## CELEBRATING DIVERSITY

I know exactly who am," said Jessica Pastron, who is fifteen. Her father is Jewish, and her mother, Japanese American. "My dad says there are many Japanese and Jewish couples. He says I'm Jewpanese. I guess, if anything, I think of myself as being white, but I don't identify myself as Jewish or Japanese. I do associate my mom with being Japanese, particularly in her habit of bringing gifts. For instance, whenever I'm spending the weekend at a friend's house, my mom will bring gifts to my friends.

"I have Asian friends, white friends. I feel I know who I am and I've always known. I've been able to move through my childhood without race defining me in any way. With some people, everything you say must be politically correct. That's boring.

"In our home we do Hanukkah and Christmas. We used to do Easter, when I still liked to color eggs. We do seder dinners with relatives. I love all the celebrations."

Like Jessica, twenty-eight-year-old Kevin believes that political correctness is a good idea gone awry. He is the German-American man who has two adopted biracial sisters, and he feels people ought to "lighten up" about race and learn to laugh. "By going through hard times with my sisters, I've learned that if you can laugh about something you can get through it. We joke about them being adopted too. For instance, we have to have the most clumsy family in the world. I think it must be genetic. When Mom or Dad stumbles or something, one of my sisters will look over at me and say, 'You're related to them.'"

Robin, twenty-nine, whose mother is white and Jewish and whose father was African American, has lived outside of the commune, where she grew up, for more than eleven years. This has been enough time to get over her shock about how widespread racism is. She agreed that a sense of humor is the best defense. So when people curious about her racial background ask, "What are you?" she generally responds, "I'm anemic." The biggest surprise, she said, was when someone responded, "You mean you came all the way over here from Anemia?"

Robin said her sister, who was also raised in the commune, uses the same approach. "She fell in love with and married this New England WASP-y guy, without telling anybody, then went back East to tell his parents, who hadn't been prepared. When my sister showed up, her new in-laws were quiet and tense. So as they sat down to dinner, my sister blurted out, 'I hope it's not a problem that I'm...' The room grew quiet as she paused, then added '...Jewish.'"

Ikuro, thirty-two, who is a blend of Native American, Scottish, Welsh, and Japanese, said despite the many difficulties she experienced as a child, she is delighted with who she is. "Having a multicultural background is like having your passport stamped around the world. You can hang out with any group and feel comfortable. Blacks, Latinos, Asians, whites—I feel like they're all my people. It's a very rich experience. I've had a chance to see up close those aspects that make us all alike.

# c h a p t e r  s i x

# WHAT WE CAN DO

*With a chapter title such as this,* the question becomes, *Why* do something? The somethings in this chapter are suggestions, some of which grow from my experiences or from those of people I interviewed. They are practical, doable steps toward making the vision of a new, more inclusive and loving world a reality—one life, one relationship, one family at a time.

## INDIVIDUALS AND COUPLES

Disconnection from our ancestors is one of the greatest losses in industrialized countries. As was discussed earlier, in the rush to become American, families often buried traditions and languages, even their names. Reconnecting with lost history emotionally can be exciting and enlightening. Although documents can be helpful, you don't have to have them or even old photographs to help you in your quest. Much of what you want to learn about ancestors is already within you, waiting to be tapped into. Here are some suggestions:

1. Research your cultural heritage, talking to relatives, pouring through family photographs, or reading up on the history of your people.

2. Establish an emotional connection to your past by writing to a known or unknown ancestor. Begin with, "Dear Great-Grandmother (or Great-Grandfather), I want to thank you for all the sacrifices you made to ensure that our family survived." With a combination of facts and/or intuitive feelings, record details of that person's life, and tell about your own. This letter will make you feel enormously grateful for your ancestral gifts. If letter writing is not you forte, draw a family tree and highlight particular strengths or constructive attitudes that were passed down to you from ancestors you know about.

3. Recognize your cultural identity. By this, I mean, "Italian American," or "European American" rather than just "white"; "Caribbean American," or "African American" rather than just

"black." And never refer to yourself as a "mutt." Honor your uniqueness.

4. If there's an elder in your family or among your in-laws who cooks a traditional ethnic dish or engages in a traditional craft, ask him or her to show you how. Besides teaching you the technique, this person might also share family stories and memories.

5. If you're about to marry, be creative about honoring deceased ancestors in your wedding. You may recall, for instance, the story of Elizabeth and Michael. She is Protestant and he is Jewish. They had a traditional chuppa, the Jewish wedding canopy, and it was made from Elizabeth's grandmother's lace tablecloth.

## ∴ CELEBRATING CULTURAL DIFFERENCES ∴

Once you have gained a firmer footing about your own cultural background, you are better prepared for learning about a partner's differences. Cultural nuances affect what we do in ways we rarely even imagine. You may recall the story of Lee and Marcy, daughter-in-law and mother-in-law, who clashed over Lee's gifts of picnic baskets. These women became closer once they shared information about their family histories and cultures. Some steps you can take to understand cultural differences include:

1. Ask questions about traditions you don't understand and, when appropriate, read books and articles with diverse views. Ignorance is not bliss.

2. Consider your lover's annoying habits or attitudes from a cultural perspective, so you don't make hasty misassumptions. Take the description "tightwad." Some traditions teach that "overspending" is sinful. Understanding doesn't necessarily mean accepting. You may remember the story of Gail, who rebelled against her Iranian husband's need for control. But as Gail also learned, "different" doesn't necessarily mean "bad." She discovered that she enjoys communal living. Her future plans call for joining a group of single professionals who will live in separate units but share a common kitchen. Some differences are opportunities for us to enhance our lives.

3. If you're converting to your mate's religion or you are both changing to one that you can jointly practice, get really clear about how you feel about what you're giving up. Talk it over with a religious advisor, your mate, your parents, and certainly with yourself.

4. If your cultural practices or attitudes are very different

from your lover's, reveal them to her. If you pray throughout the day, for instance, or feel more comfortable with certain dietary restrictions, make that clear from the start. As a matter of fact, your mate may love you all the more for your differences—assume that she will.

5. If you're planning a wedding with someone who has distinct cultural practices, don't sublimate your needs in your rush to the altar. Years from now you might feel resentful if you look back and remember that you didn't include, perhaps, a certain prayer or song for fear of offending his Aunt Sadie. By planning around your needs as well as his, your wedding will offer happy memories.

6. Compromise in advance concerning holidays and religious observances. For instance, if he observes Ramadan, the Muslim holy month, will he expect you to fast from sunrise to sunset? Or will your Jewish wife object to you putting up a Christmas tree? What will your role be as the wife of a firstborn Japanese son?

Also, if you're thinking about starting a family, include in your discussion differences in cultural attitudes concerning, for instance, raising girls and boys, which church children will attend, or how your extended family will respond to an adopted child. Use the art of compromise, but again, none of this is written in stone. Make a promise to remain open and supportive on these subjects.

7. If you're worried about bringing your new love home to dinner because you think your family will seem culturally unsophisticated or just plain ignorant, take a deep breath and tell Mama to pull out the silverware. Of course you'll want to tell your folks about significant differences in advance. But other than preparing them for something that might disturb them, let it go.

You might recall that Peter, who is Irish American, and Linda, who is Chinese American, had some tense moments when he brought her home to meet his family. Linda's family had been in the U.S. for more than a century, but his brother assumed she was a newly-arrived immigrant. Like Peter and Linda, you may look back at that first family night with laughter.

## LOVE ACROSS RACIAL LINES

If your partner is someone of a different race, here are additional guidelines that can enhance your relationship:

1. Change your attitude about those stares. One mother who has triplets said that when she's out with her darlings, everyone

gawks. The reason for that, of course, is people consider multiple births one of the last real miracles; well so is love across racial boundaries. I stare at multiracial couples all the time, and sometimes don't realize what I'm doing until I catch myself. (Then I keep at it, but in a more sneaky manner.) Assume that people are admiring you and your mate, just as they would a magnificent piece of artwork. And keep in mind that people have different opinions about the greatest works of art.

2. Be aware that few people are free of prejudice, and that means you too. A great deal of prejudice is unconscious and has been passed down to us in our families. Even if your parents never said a word against people of other races, you read their silences. Your life with your lover is an opportunity to become more accepting and open to differences. So don't be hard on yourself when you catch yourself making ridiculous assumptions.

3. When you argue with your mate, no matter how angry you may be, if you're hoping for a future together, don't call her a racist or describe something she says or does as prejudiced. She might well be narrow-minded on some subjects, but an accusation such as this will make her feel you do not appreciate sacrifices she may have made to be with you. Besides, do you really want to be the one to cast the first stone? (Remember point

two.) So learn to introduce your objections with "This is how that makes me feel" statements.

4. If your mate complains about discrimination, don't try to convince him that he misread the situation. This will only make him angrier and he'll feel unsupported. Instead, just listen. By using you as a sounding board, it will be easier to let go of the anger.

5. If you're mistreated by a landlord or employer who objects to your choice of mate, take action. Document your mistreatment and be prepared to report those actions to someone with authority or even to go to court. Taking action is a good way to handle anger, and you won't feel like a victim.

## .∴⸏. *IF FAMILY MEMBERS OBJECT TO YOUR UNION* .∴⸏.

It's not the end of the world or even your relationship with them. There's a lot you can do. Here are some suggestions:

1. Involve yourself in spiritual work that will allow you to forgive their ignorance. Forgiving doesn't mean accepting abuse, but it will give you a sense of relief. If you are spiritually inclined, a united family is certainly worth praying for.

2. If you're related to the resisting relative, give him time to

cool down. If you try to confront him right away, you both might say things that, once repeated, grow exponentially as they become part of family lore. Remember Gregor's Swedish grandmother-in-law? She took one look at his new baby girl and said, "She looks like a troll." Cruel words such as these are difficult to forget. Also, if this person refuses to participate in your wedding or other major family event, don't persist in trying to change his mind. Remember, most of the people I talked to said their relatives eventually came around.

3. If this resisting relative is a member of your family and is hurting your spouse, discuss with your partner just how much time you're both willing to give the relative to accept your union. Obviously, the amount of time required depends on physical and emotional closeness. For instance, if this is a mother who lives nearby and is able to hurt your spouse on a regular basis, it's a very different situation from having an angry big sister who lives in another town. Sometimes it's a matter of years. Many of the couples I interviewed received apologies from formerly objecting relatives after the birth of children.

4. Keep in mind that cutting ties with a close relative is a drastic step. It might mean that your children are deprived of a relationship they deserve to have. Also, you might begin to feel

resentment against your partner (no matter how unreasonably) for being the reason you can't see this relative.

5. If you have been hurt by an in-law who is resisting your relationship, write her a letter that you will never send. Pour out your hurt and anger. Say anything you wish but get your feelings out. Remember, this is for your eyes only, so don't "mistakenly" leave it around for your mate or children to see.

6. If the agreed-upon time has passed and your resisting relative has continued to hurt your spouse, take a stand. Send this relative a letter detailing how he has hurt you. Use loving language to describe what the relationship could be like, what you will miss about being with him, and what he will miss as well. In no uncertain terms, explain that if he cannot accept your partner, you are cutting off ties. Donald, the Swedish-American who is married to Janna, an African American, tried this technique and it created the results he hoped for. Donald and Janna now have the full support of both sets of in-laws.

7. If you are the mistreated spouse, don't pretend to your mate that you're not angry. Anger is a natural response to being treated unfairly. Now that you have completed writing letters to this objecting relative, you're ready to discuss your feelings with your partner. Mention no more than three examples of how this relative has hurt you and why you're angry with the relative.

Don't use this as an opportunity to point the finger at your mate. And try and refrain from using vindictive language. Once you have had your say, move on.

## ⸱∧⸜∕⸜ RAISING MULTICULTURAL CHILDREN ⸱∧⸜∕⸜⸱

The message I heard repeatedly from people invested in raising healthy multicultural children was that it is important to teach them to be proud of their uniqueness. Unfortunately, they also mentioned the importance of preparing children for hurtful situations. A lot of us avoid this because it's an admission that we can't truly protect them from all harm—and we can't. When children feel different and have no well of self-love to draw from, they feel isolated and ashamed. The goal in multicultural relationships is twofold: to help children create self-love, and to teach them about issues that concern them. Here are suggestions.

1. Familiarize your child with your ancestral language. This might include something as simple as recognizing the sound of the language on tape, memorizing words or phrases, or speaking the language fluently. Douglas Smith, a European American who is married to a Venezuelan, is enthusiastic about their sons, fourteen and twelve, speaking Spanish and English. Douglas

said, "If your children know another language it opens them up to the possibility of differences, irrespective of what the differences happen to be. Learning another language is good mental gymnastics."

Another proponent of teaching children ancestral languages is Oksana Ayoub, a Ukrainian American who married a Lebanese man who was raised in France. Oksana said it required extra effort to ensure that her children, ages eleven and thirteen, speak English, Ukrainian, and French, but she said it was well worth it. "I've always spoken Ukrainian to them, and I enrolled them in a French school until they reached the fifth grade, and now they're in an English speaking school. I believe these languages have really broadened their horizons."

2. Create a cultural scrapbook for your child. This album can be made of one of those never-used baby albums or a simple binder. Comb through old *National Geographic* magazines and travel magazines for colorful pictures, and add photocopies of family photographs. Also consider including your letter to your known or unknown ancestor. Younger children might want to draw a picture that fits this collection; older children can include school assignments on family history. Even if your child feels too "grown-up" to care about anything you put together, save it. She'll eventually treasure it.

3. Have photos of favorite or admired relatives or ancestors blown up, framed, and hung on your child's bedroom wall. At bedtime, share stories of these relatives, giving your child a sense of his cultural foundation, and point out which gifts they may have passed on to him.

4. Give your child the freedom to chose how she defines herself. By telling her she must choose one parent's culture and not the other's, you're saying she must choose one parent over another. Explain to her that the label people give her—black, white, Asian, Native, and so on—may well be different from the way she views herself. And keep in mind that the way your child identifies herself will likely change over the years. This is an essential aspect of discovering the self.

## IF YOU'RE RAISING A CHILD OF A DIFFERENT RACE

As a parent you will want to be a buffer between your child and any negative attention. Here are suggestions for handling the many aspects of this situation.

1. From a young age, talk to your children about the complications of race. Remember the story of Robin Klein, whose

mother raised her in a commune to avoid racism? She was shocked by the anger she later encountered and felt completely unprepared. Remember too Ed Guerra, a Mexican American who had German and Jewish forebears and was raised in a predominantly black and Filipino neighborhood. Ed felt so alone that he became a gang member and almost ruined his life.

2. Prepare your children for hurtful experiences. For younger children use crayons and paper to draw a picture or use dolls to prepare them for cruel words or actions. Take a doll, for instance, and tie big bundles to it that are filled with marbles and scraps of paper on which you've recorded hurtful words or beliefs. Put this heavily burdened doll beside another doll that you call by your child's name. Act out a scenario in which the heavily laden doll tries to make the other doll carry her bundles for her. Show the doll who represents your child refusing to accept them. Tell her to use words to protect herself. Have your child say through her doll, "Your angry words belong to you. I'm not taking them from you. But if you put them down, I'll play with you."

As your children grow older, use those all-important family meetings for talks and role playing so they'll know how to handle questions such as "What are you, anyway?" or insults such as "You're a Jap!" As with younger children, the goal remains the same: to teach your children not to accept the burden of someone else's prejudices. Your older child might practice saying to someone who has been offensive something such as, "What is it about *you* that makes *you* uncomfortable with who I am?"

3. If you're expecting, take photos of yourself when you're pregnant. Frame the photo and put it in a prominent place. At some point, your child might say that someone asked if she was adopted. Point to the photo, and share stories with her about how happy you were to have been pregnant with her.

4. If you have a biological or adopted child that looks different from you, prepare answers in advance to handle people who speak before they think. Try not to sound defensive. For instance, you might say, "You don't think we look alike? That's odd" or "Really? We're so close that I certainly see myself in her."

5. If you're considering adopting or stepparenting a child of a different race, you and your spouse should consider working with a therapist who can help you explore unconscious familial attitudes concerning "outsiders." Remember the story of Elise, a Eurasian, who says that even though her European-American parents believed it was God's will that they adopt her, she never felt completely accepted. There are therapists who assist with bonding between parents and adopted children. One of the most notable people is Niravi Payne who works with clients from

around the country. She can be reached at (800) 666-HEALTH.

6. If your child is adopted and someone tries to engage you in a conversation about how "lucky" or "blessed" this child was to have you save him from a terrible fate (in a war-torn country, perhaps, or foster home), turn the spirit of the message around by saying, "I'm the one who's blessed. I was longing for a little girl (or boy), and now she (or he) is in my life. I adore her (or him)."

7. If you are raising your multicultural child in a neighborhood or in a school where he is one of a handful of people of the same race, don't convince yourself that he'll be okay just as he is. Everyone needs to feel he fits in. This doesn't necessarily mean moving, but using your networking skills and creativity. If you can't find or afford a summer camp that brings together children with similar ethnic backgrounds, try posting notices on a bulletin board or web site, working to form a multicultural play group. The idea is to give your child a time he can look forward to when he'll fit in.

8. Don't confuse a cultural identity crisis with emotional issues. On a recent television talk show, a girl who had never met her African-American father and who was being raised by a loving and responsible white mother, cried as she told of being rejected by her classmates. No one on this program stopped to

address the feelings of abandonment this girl must have been grappling with over the loss of a father. Rejection from her classmates only compounded her issues. If your child is struggling, discover the real source of her problems. Blaming them on multicultural differences is a cop out.

9. If your child has hair unlike your own—too straight to curl, for instance, or too curly to comb easily—find an adult with hair like hers and ask for help. Remember that hair carries a lot of emotional weight, so treat your child's as if it's spun of gold. If your child's hair is very straight, don't apply any chemicals to try to make it curly. If it's very curly, unless she requests it, don't cut it into a closely cropped natural or have it heavily straightened. You want to make sure that you aren't sending the message that you need to "solve her problem" by "fixing" her hair. Remember that in her ancestral land, hair like hers is highly prized, and you want her to feel that way.

10. Invest in or create for yourself a painting, wall hanging, quilt, tablecloth, or any object of art that represents your "colorful" family. If you eat dinner together, pray together, and/or meet as a family, you will want this object to be near or included in some manner. The idea is for this article to later hold a special significance in your child's life that is symbolic of the beauty of your family.

II. If you're raising a child that occasionally lapses into an "urban dialect," such as Black or Chicano English, don't panic. There's an emotional connection to these languages, a way of signaling, "I'm with someone with whom I can let my guard down." Many people who associate Black English with ignorance are unaware that it is based on a systemized set of rules that can be traced back to several West African tribal languages. Black English is a melding of languages that allowed captives to communicate with one another so they could not be understood by their captors.

Chicano English, which serves as a social marker for many Mexican Americans living in the southwest region of the United States, also has a rich history and specific linguistic parameters, distinctions in pronunciation, intonation, and rhythm.

As you devise your own strategies and add to the suggestions in this chapter, remember that the bottom line for multicultural families is that what makes each of us unique can be affirmed. When that message is a theme in your household, you can build stronger relationships and raise healthy, happy children.

# C o n c l u s i o n

*When I began this book,* I thought of myself as an expert of sorts on the subject of multicultural relationships. But as I continued interviewing people, I began to realize just how little I knew and how blessed I was to have others open their lives and minds and hearts as they shared their hard-won wisdom. Perhaps most surprising of all is that because of what they told me, I've developed a higher tolerance for people who initially resist these unions. I certainly no longer think of myself as being better than they. Perhaps that's because this book has done for me what I hope it has done for you: allow you to understand people from different cultural backgrounds.

Although my mother- and father-in-law did not resist my marriage to Mark, this book has also helped me to better appreciate them, and especially our first meeting. There I was, not only someone of a different race, but a divorcée with a child. It was Christmastime, and I was carrying a gift my mother had asked for, a guitar.

It was 1982, and Mark and I had flown into Johnson City, Tennessee, together, where I stopped off to meet Audrey and Bill (where he taught at a local Christian college). I would spend the night with them before flying to my mom's home in Virginia. With the guitar slung over my shoulder, dressed in high-heeled boots, jeans, and with my hair streaming past my shoulders, I have to assume that I looked quite different from what Mark's parents had long expected their Anglo Saxon straight-as-an-arrow scholar son to bring home to mama.

As a mother who has also dreamed of the mates my children will one day bring home who will blend in "perfectly" with the rest of the family, I have been forced to consider what it must have cost Audrey and Bill emotionally, and what it cost any parent when presented to a potential family member who is different in many ways. It is so tempting to express the initial tugs of disappointment. With that in mind, I have come to appreciate the first words Audrey and Bill said to me: "Welcome to our home."

I hope that if you or your children are in a similar situation you will be greeted with warmth. But if you are not, I urge you to remember the lessons from this book: Laughter is highly important and contagious. Moments of discomfort do not a life make. People change—today's resister is a potential future best friend. And perhaps most important of all—with their resiliency, passion, and opportunities for growth—these are relationships to be celebrated. Dwell on the best moments and try to move beyond the hurtful experiences. In the meantime, may you continue to learn and grow and love throughout your lives together.

# Notes

[1] Michael Lind, "The Beige and the Black," *New York Times Magazine*, 16 August, 1998, 38.

[2] Ibid.

[3] Patrick J. McDonnell, "Immigrants Quickly Becoming Assimilated, Report Concludes," *San Francisco Chronicle*, 7 July, 1999, Sec. A, p.4.

[4] Lind, "The Beige and the Black," 38.

[5] Tamar Lewin, "New Families Redraw Racial Boundaries," *New York Times*, 27 October, 1998, Sec. A, p 19.

[6] Associated Press, "Interracial Marriages Increase," *Oakland Tribune* 26 March, 1997, Sec. A, p. 3.

[7] "The Beige and the Black," 38.

[8] Lind, "The Beige and the Black," 39.

[9] Susan Young, "Dina and Clint Eastwood: Happy with the Jet Set—Or at Home," *The Oakland Tribune,* 26 April, 1998, Sec. Cue, pp. 1-2.

[10] Susan Schindehette, Giovanna Breu and Bob Meadows, "A Fighting Chance," *People*, 29 November, 1999, 152-53.

[11] Ibid.

[12] Center for Marriage and Family, Ministry to Interchurch Marriages: "A Summary Report," Omaha, NE: Creighton University, 1999.

# About the Author

In addition to her award-winning novel, *Chesapeake Song*, which was described by *Library Journal* as "rhapsodic and eloquent," Brenda Lane Richardson has co-authored four non-fiction books, including: *What Mama Couldn't Tell Us About Love* (with Dr. Brenda Wade), *Love Lessons: A Guide to Transforming Relationships* (with Dr. Brenda Wade), *The Whole Person Fertility Program* (with Niravi Payne), and *Story Power: Talking to Teens in Turbulent Times* (with John Alston). Ms Richardson has worked as a journalist for twenty-nine years and has written for the *New York Times* and other publications. She is the recipient of numerous awards, including the Ford Foundation, Knight, and Alicia Patterson fellowships. Brenda Lane Richardson has been in an interracial marriage since 1984. She lives in New York City with her husband. They have three children and one grandchild.

# About the Press

Wildcat Canyon Press publishes books that embrace such subjects as friendship, spirituality, women's issues, and home and family, all with a focus on self-help and personal growth. Great care is taken to create books that inspire reflection and improve the quality of our lives. Our books invite sharing and are frequently given as gifts.

For a catalog of our publications, please write:

Wildcat Canyon Press

2716 Ninth Street

Berkeley, California 94710

Phone: (510) 848-3600

Fax: (510) 848-1326

info@wildcatcanyon.com

or see our website at www.wildcatcanyon.com

# More Wildcat Canyon Titles...

40 OVER 40: 40 THINGS EVERY WOMAN OVER 40 NEEDS TO KNOW ABOUT GETTING DRESSED
An image consultant shows women over forty how to love what they wear and wear what they love
*Brenda Kinsel*
$16.95 ISBN 1-885171-42-0

STILL FRIENDS: LIVING HAPPILY EVER AFTER...EVEN IF YOUR MARRIAGE FALLS APART
True stories of couples who have managed to keep their friendships intact after splitting up
*Barbara Quick*
$12.95 ISBN 1-885171-36-6

CALLING CALIFORNIA HOME: A LIVELY LOOK AT WHAT IT MEANS TO BE A CALIFORNIAN
A cornucopia of facts and trivia about Californians and the California spirit
*Heather Waite*
$14.95 ISBN 1-885171-37-4

CALLING THE MIDWEST HOME: A LIVELY LOOK AT THE ORIGINS, ATTITUDES, QUIRKS, AND CURIOSITIES OF AMERICAN'S HEARTLANDERS
A loving look at the people who call the Midwest home—whether they live there or not
*Carolyn Lieberg*
$14.95 ISBN 1-885171-12-9

I WAS MY MOTHER'S BRIDESMAID: YOUNG ADULTS TALK ABOUT THRIVING IN A BLENDED FAMILY
The truth about growing up in a "combined family."
*Erica Carlisle and Vanessa Carlisle*
$13.95 ISBN 1-885171-34-X

THE COURAGE TO BE A STEPMOM: FINDING YOUR PLACE WITHOUT LOSING YOURSELF
Hands-on advice and emotional support for stepmothers.
*Sue Patton Thoele*
$14.95 ISBN 1-885171-28-5

CELEBRATING FAMILY: OUR LIFELONG BONDS WITH PARENTS AND SIBLINGS
True stories about how baby boomers have recognized the flaws of their families
and come to love them as they are.
*Lisa Braver Moss*
$13.95 ISBN 1-885171-30-7

AUNTIES: OUR OLDER, COOLER, WISER FRIENDS
An affectionate tribute to the unique and wonderful women we call "Auntie."
*Tamara Traeder and Julienne Bennett*
$12.95 ISBN 1-885171-22-6

THE AUNTIES KEEPSAKE BOOK: THE STORY OF OUR FRIENDSHIP
A beautiful way to tell the wonderful story of you and your auntie or niece
*Tamara Traeder and Julienne Bennett*
$19.95 ISBN 1-885171-29-3

LITTLE SISTERS: THE LAST BUT NOT THE LEAST
A feisty look at the trials and tribulations, joys and advantages of being a little
sister.
*Carolyn Lieberg*
$13.95 ISBN 1-885171-24-2

girlfriends: INVISIBLE BONDS, ENDURING TIES
Filled with true stories of ordinary women and extraordinary friendships,
*girlfriends* has become a gift of love among women everywhere.
*Carmen Renee Berry and Tamara Traeder*
$12.95 ISBN 1-885171-08-0
Also Available: Hardcover gift edition, $20.00 ISBN 1-885171-20-X

girlfriends FOR LIFE: FRIENDSHIPS WORTH KEEPING FOREVER
This follow-up to the best-selling *girlfriends* is an all-new collection of stories and anecdotes about the amazing bonds of women's friendships.
*Carmen Renee Berry and Tamara Traeder*
$13.95 ISBN 1-885171-32-3

THE girlfriends KEEPSAKE BOOK: THE STORY OF OUR FRIENDSHIP
A unique way to celebrate the bond of friendship.
*Carmen Renee Berry and Tamara Traeder*
$19.95 ISBN 1-885171-13-7

AND WHAT DO YOU DO? WHEN WOMEN CHOOSE TO STAY HOME
At last, a book for the 7.72 million married women who don't work outside the home—by choice!
*Loretta Kaufman and Mary Quigley*
$14.95 ISBN 1-885171-40-4

A COUPLE OF FRIENDS: THE REMARKABLE FRIENDSHIP BETWEEN STRAIGHT WOMEN AND GAY MEN
What makes the friendships between straight women and gay men so wonderful? Find out in this honest and fascinating book.
*Robert H. Hopcke and Laura Rafaty*
$14.95 ISBN 1-885171-33-1

INDEPENDENT WOMEN: CREATING OUR LIVES, LIVING OUR VISIONS
How women value independence and relationship and are redefining their lives to accommodate both.
*Debra Sands Miller*
$16.95 ISBN 1-885171-25-0

THE WORRYWART'S COMPANION: TWENTY-ONE WAYS TO SOOTHE YOURSELF AND WORRY SMART
The perfect gift for anyone who lies awake at night worrying.
*Dr. Beverly Potter*
$11.95 ISBN 1-885171-15-3

OUT OF THE BLUE: ONE WOMAN'S STORY OF STROKE, LOVE, AND SURVIVAL
A candid and inspirational account with the pace of a thriller
*Bonnie Sherr Klein*
$15.95 ISBN 1-885171-45-5

BREASTS: OUR MOST PUBLIC PRIVATE PARTS
A revealing look at what women really think and feel
*Meema Spadola*
$13.95 ISBN 1-885171-27-7

THOSE WHO CAN...TEACH!: CELEBRATING TEACHERS WHO MAKE A DIFFERENCE
Stories of tribute to a broad range of men and women who change lives
*Lorraine Glennon and Mary Mohler*
$!2.95 ISBN 1-885171-35-8

DIAMONDS OF THE NIGHT: THE SEARCH FOR SPIRIT IN YOUR DREAMS
Sixteen principles distilled out of a therapist's work with the power of dreams
*James Hagan, Ph.D.*
$16.95 ISBN 1-879290-12-X

Books are available at fine retailers nationwide.

Prices subject to change without notice.